Contemporary Vocabulary

Contemporary Vocabulary

Elliott L. Smith

St. Martin's Press　　NEW YORK

Library of Congress Catalog Card Number: 78-65215

Copyright © 1979 by St. Martin's Press, Inc.

All Rights Reserved.

Manufactured in the United States of America.

32109

fedcb

For information, write St. Martin's Press, Inc.,
175 Fifth Avenue, New York, N. Y. 10010

cover design: Jack McCurdy

typography: Patricia Smythe

ISBN: 0-312-16847-0

Preface

     Contemporary Vocabulary has been developed over a period of more than fifteen years, during which time the materials have been refined by the responses of several thousand students. Generally, it is intended as a practical workbook for beginning college students who recognize a need to improve their vocabularies in order to read with greater understanding and write and speak more effectively. But eleventh and twelfth graders looking forward to college and even college juniors and seniors facing graduate school or gainful employment have also benefited from the book's sequences of exercises. The words included are not esoteric but are part of the regular vocabulary of undergraduate college textbooks, newspapers, and such magazines as *Time, Newsweek,* and *U. S. News and World Report.*

     The book is divided into two parts, each with a self-scored pretest and posttest. (Other quizzes are provided in the Instructor's Manual.) Part One, "Word Elements," teaches students to unlock the meanings of words through an understanding of Latin and Greek roots (chapters 1 and 2), prefixes (chapter 3), and suffixes (chapter 4). For many users of the book, these chapters will be the most important. They offer the greatest potential increase in word power for the time invested, since many tens of thousands of English words are based wholly or partially on the approximately two hundred elements with which students become familiar as they work through the exercises.

     In Part Two, the emphasis shifts from the mastery of elements to improving the students' facility with particular types of words. Chapters 5 and 6 deal with what I have called "action words" and "descriptive words"—words that not only occur frequently in college reading but lend strength, precision, and variety to student writing. Since many of these words contain Latin and Greek roots, prefixes, and suffixes, the study of these chapters also reinforces what has been learned in Part One. The final two chapters (7 and 8) introduce words derived from names (eponyms) and foreign expressions commonly used in English. These chapters are perhaps the least fundamental (under constraints of time some instructors may wish to skip them), but some of my students—especially those with better than average preparation—have found them the most interesting.

     The strength of *Contemporary Vocabulary* is its method of instruction. Each chapter contains sequences of exercises in which students are given the opportunity to do just about everything that can be done with words. In Part One, for example, students pronounce words, compare them with similar words, study current definitions, answer true-false questions about them, insert them into sentences, match them with definitions, and finally construct sentences around them. The method, then, is usage, and the assumption behind the method is that multiple reinforcement not only helps students remember what words mean but enables them to use the words in sentences of their own. In Part Two the sequences include crisscross puzzles and variations on the sentence fill-in and matching exercises encountered in Part One. Throughout the book there is enough variety among the exercise sequences to avoid tedium, but there is also sufficient repetition of format to prevent confusion.

About pronunciation: To ignore it, as some texts do, or to argue its importance and then expect students to look up every pronunciation in a dictionary, as other texts do, seems to me a terrible waste of an opportunity—for a very slight additional investment of time and space—to put every word fully at the student's command, for purposes of speaking and listening as well as writing and reading. Yet the texts that laudably do offer pronunciations generally suffer from systems of notation that are either so oversimplified that they do not accurately represent the sounds of English or so complicated that they cannot be readily kept in mind and used. *Contemporary Vocabulary* steers past these hazards. For every word studied it gives a pronunciation, consistently employing a system of notation that is both as simple and as complex as it needs to be. I have found that students master the system quickly and easily, and for convenient reference I have repeated a pronunciation key at the bottom of every page on which pronunciations appear. A final problem with suggesting pronunciations is that there is, of course, no one absolutely right and perfect way to pronounce a word. There are regional and other variations to which no text could possibly do justice. The only feasible approach is to alert the student emphatically to this important fact, as I do on page 2, and then to go on and offer a pronunciation that will be generally acceptable. Every pronunciation in *Contemporary Vocabulary* has been checked against at least three reputable dictionaries.

Contemporary Vocabulary is hardly the product of my efforts alone. I have mentioned my debt to the thousands of students who have honed the exercises through the years. I wish to acknowledge the patient and professional guidance of the people at St. Martin's Press, Nancy Perry in particular. I am also indebted to Glorya Cohen for her meticulous copy editing of the manuscript. Among my colleagues at Ferris State College, I wish to thank Mary Bower, Keitha Breault, Ann Breitenwischer, Sara Krumins, and Elaine Nienhouse of the library staff for their research assistance and encouragement; Donald Hanzek for his help with the foreign phrases chapter; Joseph Dugas for his experienced counsel as well as the use of his personal library; and Andrew Hart for his perceptive criticism of every aspect of the book. But I must reserve my greatest acknowledgment of debt for my wife, Wanda, because without her unflagging support and day-to-day assistance, the project would have been abandoned long ago.

Elliott L. Smith

Contents

Contemporary Vocabulary

PART ONE

WORD ELEMENTS

Words are made up of component parts called roots or bases, prefixes, and suffixes. A word's *root* may be thought of as its kernel or nucleus, the part that can be increased or enlarged by the addition of prefixes and suffixes. The following chart demonstrates how words are assembled:

prefix		root		suffix		word
a-	+	the	+	-ism	=	atheism
an-	+	onym	+	-ous	=	anonymous
con-	+	greg	+	-ation	=	congregation
de-	+	mot	+	-ion	=	demotion
ec-	+	centr	+	-ic	=	eccentric
im-	+	migr	+	-ate	=	immigrate
in-	+	flu	+	-ence	=	influence
para-	+	med	+	-ic	=	paramedic
trans-	+	miss	+	-ion	=	transmission
tri-	+	enni	+	-al	=	triennial

Roots, prefixes, and suffixes should not be confused with *syllables,* which are simply uninterrupted clusters of sounds (usually containing a vowel) in spoken words. You will find that many prefixes, roots, and suffixes contain more than one syllable. Typical examples include the prefixes *circum-, extra-, macro-,* and *multi-;* the roots *amat, audit, capit, fratern, liber,* and *lumin;* and the suffixes *-able, -ation, -escent,* and *-istic.*

1

There are also times when words contain more than one root. When this occurs, the roots may be called *combining forms.* Some examples of combining forms are shown in the chart that follows:

root		root		suffix		word
aqua	+	mar	+	-ine	=	aquamarine
bene	+	dict	+	-ion	=	benediction
bio	+	gen	+	-esis	=	biogenesis
carni	+	vor	+	-ous	=	carnivorous
cent	+	enni	+	-al	=	centennial
equi	+	vocat	+	-ion	=	equivocation
omni	+	pot	+	-ence	=	omnipotence
phil	+	anthrop	+	-y	=	philanthropy
tele	+	vis	+	-ion	=	television
veri	+	simil	+	-itude	=	verisimilitude

To be comfortable with a word, especially a word new to you, you must know more than its construction. You should be able to pronounce it with confidence. The study of word pronunciation is called *phonics.* Phonics can be complicated because people tend to pronounce words as they are taught to pronounce them by their peers, the people around them. It must be understood that there is no absolutely right and perfect way to pronounce any word. For example, a well-educated person in Alabama might pronounce such words as "bright," "contemporary," "laboratory," and "fasten" quite differently from an equally well-educated person in, say, Boston or London. Nevertheless, to learn to pronounce words new to us, we must strike some midpoint. The following pronunciation key is the one used throughout *Contemporary Vocabulary:*

a (*a*sk, f*a*t, br*a*t)
ay (*a*pe, f*a*te, g*ay*)
ah (f*a*r, f*a*ther, *o*n)
*âh (French, between a and ah)
au (*ou*t, d*ou*bt, l*ou*sy, c*ow*)
b (*b*ite, ta*b*le, fi*b*)
ch (*ch*eat, *ch*ur*ch*, ar*ch*)
d (*d*og, nee*d*le, so*d*)
e (s*e*lf, b*ee*n, c*a*re)
ee (*e*qual, h*ea*t, hon*ey*)
*ê (French, between o and e)
ə (*a*bout, *a*gent, circ*u*s)
f (*f*lag, a*f*ter, *ph*one)
g (*g*o, ha*gg*le, lo*g*)
h (*h*er, a*h*ead, *h*ome)
hw (*wh*ile, *wh*en, no*wh*ere)
i (*i*f, k*i*t, m*i*rror)
iy (*i*ce, k*i*te, den*y*)
j (*j*ump, a*g*ile, fu*dg*e)

k (*k*iss, ca*k*e, sha*k*e)
l (*l*ow, fe*ll*ow, leve*l*)
m (*m*e, ca*m*el, *m*u*m*)
n (*n*o, a*nn*ul, fa*n*)
ŋ (li*n*k, a*n*ger, si*ng*)
o (*au*dio, f*a*ll, c*o*rn)
ow (*o*ver, l*o*tion, sh*ow*)
oo (b*oo*k, b*u*ll, p*oo*r)
*ô (European, between ow and ay)
oi (*oi*l, s*oi*l, j*oi*nt, j*oy*)
p (*p*un, gra*pp*le, tra*p*)
r (*r*un, spo*r*t, fea*r*)
s (*s*in, *c*enter, wre*s*tle, hara*ss*)
sh (*sh*oe, ambi*t*ion, sma*sh*)
t (*t*own, ra*tt*le, ca*t*)
th (*th*ink, e*th*er, tru*th*)
t̂h (*th*is, wi*th*er, la*the*)
u (*u*p, h*u*t, b*u*rn, det*e*r)
*û (European, between uw and ee)

uw (*ooze, lose, shoe, fool*) yu (b*ure*au, p*ure*)
v (*v*an, sho*v*el, sa*v*e) yuw (*u*nited, *youth*, p*u*ke, sk*ew*)
w (*w*e, a*w*ay, s*w*erve) z (*z*inc, da*zz*le, ma*z*e)
y (*y*es, on*i*on, law*y*er) zh (plea*s*ure, mea*s*ure, lei*s*ure)

The characters marked with an asterisk (*) represent sounds considered foreign to the English language. They will be explained in detail in the introduction to the chapter "Foreign Expressions in English."

When you first look at this alphabet, it may appear terribly complex, but in fact it is far simpler than the English spelling system that all of us struggle with daily. For example, in traditional English spelling, the *sh* sound may be spelled at least thirteen different ways. As the chart below shows, our phonic alphabet spells the sound only one way—*sh:*

English Spelling	*Phonic Spelling*
con*sci*ence	(KAHN-shən)
ma*ch*ine	(mə-SHEEN)
man*si*on	(MAN-shən)
men*ti*on	(MEN-shən)
mi*ss*ion	(MISH-ən)
nau*se*ous	(NO-shəs)
o*ce*an	(OW-shən)
p*sh*aw	(SHO)
*sch*ist	(SHIST)
*sh*ow	(SHOW)
spe*ci*al	(SPESH-əl)
*s*ugar	(SHOOG-ər)
ti*ss*ue	(TISH-uw)

The English system also spells parts of words the same way and then pronounces them differently. Note the *ough* grouping in the following chart:

English Spelling	*Phonic Spelling*
cough	(KOF)
hiccough	(HIK-əp)
plough	(PLAU)
though	(THOW)
through	(THRUW)
tough	(TUF)

Our phonic alphabet, then, is intended to spell words out so that you can learn to pronounce them quickly. The same sounds are consistently represented by the same characters, yet the system retains as many of our traditional letters as possible. The system has three levels of stress. The strongest, or primary stress, is indicated by CAPITAL LETTERS; the secondary stress is indicated by *italics*; and the third, or tertiary stress, is indicated by ordinary characters. The following chart contains words that demonstrate these stress patterns:

3

English Spelling	*Phonic Spelling*
acrobat	(AK-rə-*bat*)
agriculture	(AG-rə-*kul*-chər)
bribery	(BRIY-bər-ee)
captivate	(KAP-tə-*vayt*)
eternity	(i-TUR-nə-tee)
homogenize	(hə-MAHJ-ə-*niyz*)
instantaneous	(*in*-stən-TAY-nee-əs)
photographic	(*fow*-tə-GRAF-ik)
unanimous	(yuw-NAN-ə-məs)
zodiac	(ZOW-dee-*ak*)

As an exercise, try to write in ordinary spelling the following words given in our phonic alphabet:

1. (*mis*-ə-SIP-ee) _____

2. (KRIS-məs) _____

3. (*pen*-ə-SIL-in) _____

4. (bi-KEE-nee) _____

5. (ri-VAHL-viŋ) _____

6. (BUT-ər-*fliy*) _____

7. (vow-KAB-yə-*ler*-ee) _____

8. (mə-LISH-əs) _____

9. (HWIS-əl) _____

10. (byuw-TISH-ən) _____

11. (KAHL-ij) _____

12. (LAHB-stər) _____

13. (ə-LAU-əns) _____

14. (KWIK-*sand*) _____

15. (*pen*-ə-TEN-shə-ree) _____

The answers are: 1. *Mississippi*, 2. *Christmas*, 3. *penicillin*, 4. *bikini*, 5. *revolving*, 6. *butterfly*, 7. *vocabulary*, 8. *malicious*, 9. *whistle*, 10. *beautician*, 11. *college*, 12. *lobster*, 13. *allowance*, 14. *quicksand*, 15. *penitentiary*.

Before moving on to the individual chapters on roots, prefixes, and suffixes, we will pause for a self-scoring pretest. This test will give you an idea of the level of difficulty of the words to be taken up in Part One. The answers follow the test.

Self-scoring Pretest

MULTIPLE CHOICE

Place the letter of the best answer in the blank space.

_____ 1. An *amorist* is likely to be an expert at
   a. finance
   b. love-making
   c. public debate
   d. military strategy

_____ 2. A *superannuated* person is
   a. hostile
   b. immature
   c. old
   d. penniless

_____ 3. *Avian* characteristics are
   a. hospitable
   b. naive
   c. suggestive of death
   d. birdlike

_____ 4. An *incarnate* creature is one who is
   a. fiendishly evil
   b. hideously misshapen
   c. in bodily form
   d. approaching death

_____ 5. A *centenarian* is
   a. a celebration
   b. a military hero
   c. a legal statement
   d. an aged person

_____ 6. A person without *credibility* is
   a. untrustworthy
   b. insolvent
   c. very emotional
   d. commonplace

_____ 7. A *fiduciary* is a
   a. relative
   b. priest
   c. trustee
   d. fortune-teller

_____ 8. A *confraternity* is a
   a. subversive political party
   b. unified group of people
   c. class reunion
   d. collection of immigrants

_____ 9. *Egregious* behavior is likely to be
   a. polite
   b. shocking
   c. irrational
   d. clever

_____ 10. A *rejoinder* is a
   a. military person
   b. type of weld
   c. clever reply
   d. stupid blunder

_____ 11. *Perjury* involves
   a. doing good for others
   b. a careful avoidance of mistakes
   c. dressing according to the latest style
   d. lying under oath

_____ 12. *Loquacious* individuals are often
   a. moody
   b. jealous
   c. taciturn
   d. talkative

5

5. My *annuity* payments are no longer _____

_____

6. *Aqua* tints highlighted _____

_____

7. The *artifice* of the villain amazed _____

_____

8. One of the *perennial* arguments between the faculty and the administration involves

_____

9. An *armada* of miniature sailboats _____

_____

10. The *artifacts* of modern civilization may _____

_____

11. An uneasy *armistice* was declared when _____

_____

12. The *aqueous* compound was _____

_____

Words from Latin Roots (3)

ROOTS

1. *aud(it)* (hear, listen): auditorium _____

2. *avi* (bird): aviation _____

3. *bell(i)* (war): rebellion _____

4. *ben(e)* (good, well): benefit _____

WORD LIST

1. ante*bell*um (*an*-tee-BEL-əm): before the war, especially the American Civil War
2. *audit*ion (ə-DISH-ən): a hearing, as a test for an actor or musician
3. *audit*ory (O-də-*tor*-ee): related to the sense of hearing
4. *avi*an (AY-vee-ən): characteristic of or pertaining to birds
5. *avi*ary (AY-vee-*er*-ee): an elaborate structure for housing birds
6. *avi*onics (*ay*-vee-AHN-iks): the technology of electronic aviation equipment
7. *bell*icose (BEL-ə-*kows*): eager to fight; generally quarrelsome
8. *bell*igerency (bə-LIJ-ər-ən-see): the condition of warlike hostility; a hostile action
9. *bene*factor (BEN-ə-*fak*-tər): a person who gives another (financial) help; a patron
10. *bene*ficiary (*ben*-ə-FISH-ee-*er*-ee): one who receives the benefit of payment, as from an insurance policy
11. *ben*ign (bi-NIYN): not malignant; gracious and kindly; good-natured
12. in*audi*ble (in-O-də-bəl): cannot be heard (by the human ear)

TRUE-FALSE

_____ 1. *Avionics* is a branch of ornithology.

_____ 2. *Auditory* stimulations most affect the sense of taste.

_____ 3. A person with a *benign* temperament is likely to be good-natured and easygoing.

---

a (*f*at);   ay (*f*ate);   ah (*f*ar);   au (*dou*bt);   ch (*ch*ur*ch*);   e (*se*lf, *ca*re);   ee (*e*vening);   ə (*a*bout);   f (*f*lag, *ph*one);   hw (*wh*ile);   i (*f*it);   iy (*k*ite);   ŋ (li*nk*, si*ng*);   o (*au*dio, *c*orn);   ow (*o*pen);   oo (*c*ook);   oi (*oi*l);   sh (*sh*oe, ambi*ti*on);   th (*th*ink);   u (*u*p, l*o*ve);   uw (*oo*ze);   yu (c*u*re);   yuw (*youth*, *u*nited);   zh (plea*s*ure)

19

_____ 4. We normally think of a *benefactor* as an archenemy.

_____ 5. A *belligerency* is an act of kindness.

_____ 6. One of the purposes of an *audition* may be to discover new talent.

_____ 7. Flight is an *avian* characteristic.

_____ 8. *Bellicose* individuals generally make the best diplomats.

_____ 9. A *beneficiary* is a tax collector.

_____10. An *aviary* ordinarily houses a whole array of barnyard animals.

_____11. Cotton was the agricultural king in the *antebellum* South.

_____12. If a sound is *inaudible,* you can't hear it.

SENTENCE FILL-IN

1. This whistle makes a sound _____ to the human ear.

2. The speaker from the Audubon Society called the enormous bird cage an

   _____ .

3. I was more surprised than anyone else to learn that I was a _____ of my uncle's will.

4. Though once stately, the _____ homes of Memphis are today in a deteriorating condition.

5. An obvious _____ in the speaker's tone made it clear that he wanted to convince his listeners to go to war.

6. With the steadily increasing number of private pilots, _____ equipment becomes ever more vital for public safety.

7. Tom insists on calling his _____ his meal ticket.

8. More than a hundred performers came to the theater to _____ for only three parts.

9. Everyone was relieved to learn that Mother's tumor was _____ .

10. When we are children, most of us have fantastic dreams of _____ flights across the sky.

11. The ambassador's _____ pronouncements hardly seemed designed to promote peace.

12. A gradual reduction in _____ sensitivity has left Graham almost deaf.

MATCHING

_____ 1. in*aud*ible

_____ 2. ante*bell*um

_____ 3. *ben*ign

_____ 4. *audit*ion

_____ 5. *bene*ficiary

_____ 6. *audit*ory

_____ 7. *bene*factor

_____ 8. *avi*an

_____ 9. *belli*gerency

_____10. *avi*ary

_____11. *belli*cose

_____12. *avi*onics

a. a person who gives another (financial) help; a patron
b. related to the sense of hearing
c. an elaborate structure for housing birds
d. the condition of warlike hostility; a hostile action
e. cannot be heard (by the human ear)
f. before the war, especially the American Civil War
g. the technology of electronic aviation equipment
h. a hearing, as a test for an actor or musician
i. not malignant; gracious and kindly; good-natured
j. characteristic of or pertaining to birds
k. eager to fight; generally quarrelsome
l. one who receives the benefit of payment, as from an insurance policy

SENTENCE COMPLETION

1. An almost *inaudible* buzzing came from _____

_____

2. A *bellicose* tribe of troublemakers came _____

_____

3. With *avian* intensity, Clifford glared at _____

_____

4. The *auditions* lasted from _____

_____

5. A more *benign* approach to student problems might _____

_____

6. The rebel's overt *belligerency* led to _____

_____

21

7. At the zoo we saw an *aviary* in which _____

_____

8. The estate's first three *beneficiaries* suddenly began to _____

_____

9. An *antebellum* nostalgia has _____

_____

10. Benedict's *auditory* hallucinations began shortly after _____

_____

11. My *benefactor* insists that _____

_____

12. An *aviation* historian, Gretchen can tell _____

_____

Words from Latin Roots (4)

ROOTS

1. *bon, boun* (good): bonus, bounty _____

2. *capit, capt* (head, chief): capital, captain _____

3. *carn (i)* (flesh): carnation _____

4. *ced(e), ceed, cess* (go, yield, surrender): recede, proceed, success _____

DERIVATIVES

1. ac*ced*e (ak-SEED):   to give in to; to assume official responsibility
2. *bon*a fide (BOW-nə-*fiyd*):   the real thing; in good faith
3. *bon*anza (bə-NAN-zə):   a sudden and unexpected source of money or riches
4. *boun*teous (BAUN-tee-əs):   inclined to be generous; plentiful and abundant
5. *capit*alize (KAP-ə-təl-*iyz*):   to turn to (one's) advantage or profit
6. *capit*ulation (kə-*pich*-ə-LAY-shən):   a surrendering, usually upon prearranged terms or conditions
7. *carn*age (KAHR-nij):   a great slaughter, as in a battle
8. *carni*vorous (kahr-NIV-ər-əs):   flesh-eating, as an animal
9. in*carn*ate (in-KAHR-nit):   in the flesh; in bodily form
10. pre*ced*ent (PRES-ə-dənt):   a previous act (decision) taken as a valid model
11. re*capit*ulation (*ree*-kə-*pich*-ə-LAY-shən):   a brief repetition made in order to remind
12. re*cess*ion (ri-SESH-ən):   a backing up or withdrawing; a time of slow economic activity

TRUE-FALSE

_____ 1. A *capitulation* usually involves ignoring all challenges and going your own way.

_____ 2. A *bonanza* is likely to prove profitable or bountiful.

---

a (f*a*t); ay (f*a*te); ah (f*a*r); au (d*ou*bt); ch (*ch*ur*ch*); e (s*e*lf, c*a*re); ee (*e*vening); ə (*a*bout); f (*f*lag; *ph*one); hw (*wh*ile); i (f*i*t); iy (k*i*te); ŋ (li*n*k, si*ng*); o (*au*dio, c*o*rn); ow (*o*pen); oo (c*oo*k); oi (*oi*l); sh (*sh*oe, ambi*ti*on); th (*th*ink); u (*u*p, l*o*ve); uw (*oo*ze); yu (c*u*re); yuw (*you*th, *u*nited); zh (plea*s*ure)

4. An administrative staff grown *corpulent* from lack of good management practices eventually faces _____

_____

5. A great *concourse* of refugees came toward _____

_____

6. The revolutionary's *credo* denounced _____

_____

7. If we can *incorporate* the best points of both plans into one proposal, we can _____

_____

8. Three tiny *denticles* were _____

_____

9. For a politician, *credibility* is _____

_____

10. The *corporal* remains of the explosion victims _____

_____

11. The *dentifrice* was so abrasive that _____

_____

12. After a *cursory* appraisal of the situation, I _____

_____

Words from Latin Roots (7)

ROOTS

1. *dic*(*t*) (say, tell): diction _____

2. *duc*(*t*), *duce* (lead): conduct, induce _____

   _____

3. *fid, fed* (faith, trust): confident, federal _____

   _____

4. *fin* (end, limit): finish _____

WORD LIST

1. aque*duct* (AK-wə-*dukt*): a large pipe for moving water or liquid waste material
2. bene*dic*tion (*ben*-ə-DIK-shən): the invocation of a divine blessing
3. con*duc*ive (kən-DUW-siv): tending to lead, help, or assist
4. con*fed*erate (kən-FED-ər-it): an accomplice (in some criminal enterprise)
5. de*duc*tive (di-DUK-tiv): related to reasoning that begins with a known premise and works to a conclusion
6. de*fin*itive (di-FIN-ə-tiv): completely accurate, reliable, and authoritative
7. *dict*um (DIK-təm): an authoritative saying or maxim
8. *fid*elity (fə-DEL-ə-tee): faithfulness to one's promise or obligations
9. *fid*uciary (fi-DUW-shee-*er*-ee): an individual who holds something in trust for another; a trustee
10. *fin*ale (fi-NAH-lee): a "grand" conclusion
11. *fin*ite (FIY-*niyt*): limited (bordered) by time
12. in*dic*ative (in-DIK-ə-tiv): characteristic of or very much like

---

a (*fat*); ay (*fate*); ah (*far*); au (*doubt*); ch (*church*); e (*self, care*); ee (*evening*); ə (*about*); f (*flag, phone*); hw (*while*); i (*fit*); iy (*kite*); ŋ (*link, sing*); o (*audio, corn*); ow (*open*); oo (*cook*); oi (*oil*); sh (*shoe, ambition*); th (*think*); u (*up, love*); uw (*ooze*); yu (*cure*); yuw (*youth, united*); zh (*pleasure*)

TRUE-FALSE

_____ 1. Personal *fidelity* must include trustworthiness.

_____ 2. A *benediction* usually requests general destruction of one's enemies.

_____ 3. One normally expects the *finale* to come at the end.

_____ 4. One's *confederate* is a dangerous and untrustworthy stool pigeon.

_____ 5. An *aqueduct* is an amphibious vehicle.

_____ 6. *Deductive* statements are always false.

_____ 7. A *definitive* interpretation is likely to be a complete one.

_____ 8. A *dictum* is a diamond-pointed phonograph needle.

_____ 9. Anything *conducive* to living a long life is likely to be good for you.

_____10. Any remark *indicative* of the truth must be false.

_____11. A *fiduciary* is likely to handle some of your money for you.

_____12. All *finite* creatures must eventually face the prospect of death.

SENTENCE FILL-IN

1. The chauvinist's opening remarks were clearly _____ of how little he thought of most women.

2. One of the most _____ works on Bach was written by the great human-itarian Albert Schweitzer.

3. Tons of liquefied waste pass through the disposal _____ daily.

4. The earth contains only a _____ store of fossil fuels.

5. It is part of a guru's profession to have a convincing _____ ready for every occasion.

6. The _____ of the *1812 Overture* is usually accompanied by the firing of cannons.

7. Our national interest in all things scientific is _____ to the development of new products.

8. The family _____ held the money in trust for the heirs until they became eighteen.

9. The accused admitted having at least one _____ in the scheme.

10. The padre's _____ was longer than his sermon.

11. The report maintained that _____ to the marriage vows is not as widespread as it was thirty years ago.

12. The _____ process begins with a general statement believed to be factual.

MATCHING

_____ 1. in*dic*ative

_____ 2. aque*duct*

_____ 3. *fin*ite

_____ 4. bene*dict*ion

_____ 5. *fin*ale

_____ 6. con*duc*ive

_____ 7. *fid*uciary

_____ 8. con*fed*erate

_____ 9. *fid*elity

_____10. de*duct*ive

_____11. *dict*um

_____12. de*fin*itive

a. an accomplice (in some criminal enterprise)
b. a large pipe for moving water or liquid waste material
c. related to reasoning that begins with a known premise and works to a conclusion
d. completely accurate, reliable, and authoritative
e. the invocation of a divine blessing
f. characteristic of or very much like
g. an individual who holds something in trust for another; a trustee
h. limited (bordered) by time
i. faithfulness to one's promise or obligations
j. tending to lead, help, or assist
k. a "grand" conclusion
l. an authoritative saying or maxim

SENTENCE COMPLETION

1. *Deductive* reasoning can be very helpful when _____

_____

2. Such a silly *dictum* _____

_____

3. We are in search of a *definitive* explanation of _____

_____

4. At least one of the *confederates* in the enterprise admitted that _____

_____

37

5. I don't understand how such a plan would be *conducive* to _____

_____

6. An untrustworthy *fiduciary* can _____

_____

7. Our monthly sales figures are only *indicative* of _____

_____

8. The *finale* of the celebration included _____

_____

9. The installation of a new *aqueduct* may _____

_____

10. Wesley's *fidelity* to company policy will _____

_____

11. After the *benediction,* everyone _____

_____

12. When we become aware of just how *finite* we are, we sometimes _____

_____

Words from Latin Roots (8)

ROOTS

1. *flect, flex* (bend, turn): deflect, reflex _____

2. *flu(x)* (flow): fluid, influx _____

3. *fort, forc* (strong): fortify, forceful _____

   _____

4. *frater(n), fratr* (brother): fraternity _____

WORD LIST

1. af*flu*ent (AF-luw-ənt): flowing with wealth and abundance; prosperous
2. con*flu*ence (KAHN-fluw-əns): a running or flowing together, as rivers or ideas
3. con*fratern*ity (*kahn*-frə-TUR-nə-tee): a society (of men) united for a specific purpose
4. *flex*uous (FLEK-shuw-əs): winding in and out; bending or wavering
5. *fort*e (for-TAY): one's special area of accomplishment
6. *fort*itude (FOR-tə-*tuwd*): strength of character; patient courage
7. *fort*uitous (for-TUW-ə-təs): happening by the chance of good luck; unplanned
8. *fratern*ize (FRAT-ər-*niyz*): to mix together (socialize) in a brotherly fashion; to associate with
9. *fratr*icide (FRA-trə-*siyd*): the killing of a brother, or one who commits such an act
10. genu*flect* (JEN-yə-*flekt*): to drop to one knee in a prayer position
11. in*flect*ion (in-FLEK-shən): a slight change in tone or modulation of the voice; a point of emphasis
12. super*flu*ous (soo-PUR-fluw-əs): (flowing) beyond what is needed; needlessly abundant

TRUE-FALSE

_____ 1. A *confraternity* is a collection of people who are alienated from one another.

_____ 2. *Fortuitous* planning is practically no planning at all.

---

a (*f*a*t*); ay (*f*a*t*e); ah (*f*a*r*); au (*d*o*u*bt); ch (*ch*ur*ch*); e (*s*e*lf, c*a*re*); ee (*ev*ening); ə (*a*bout); f (*f*lag, *ph*one); hw (*wh*ile); i (*f*i*t*); iy (*k*i*t*e); ŋ (li*n*k, si*ng*); o (*au*dio, c*o*rn); ow (*o*pen); oo (c*oo*k); oi (*oi*l); sh (*sh*oe, ambi*ti*on); th (*th*ink); u (*u*p, l*o*ve); uw (*oo*ze); yu (c*u*re); yuw (*y*outh, *u*nited); zh (plea*s*ure)

_____ 3. To *fraternize* is to associate on a friendly basis.

_____ 4. For an *inflection* to be most effective, it should go unnoticed.

_____ 5. A *confluence* involves a coming together.

_____ 6. You would hardly expect an alcoholic's *forte* to be high-wire walking.

_____ 7. A *flexuous* stance is unsteady and uncertain.

_____ 8. *Superfluous* goods are absolutely vital to existence.

_____ 9. We normally think of *fortitude* as emotional fickleness.

_____10. *Affluent* people are expected to buy their groceries with food stamps.

_____11. One is likely to *genuflect* in a cathedral.

_____12. The concept of *fratricide* is based on the notion of increased brotherly love.

SENTENCE FILL-IN

1. After failing advanced composition for the second time, Owen admitted that language study had never been his _____.

2. My brother has repeatedly suggested that I not _____ with such shady characters.

3. After the convention was over, the whole thing seemed to me to have been a _____ mass of words.

4. By the slightest _____ of his voice, a great actor can hold his audience.

5. A considerable measure of _____ will be required to withstand the opposition that is certain to fall upon us.

6. All warfare can be thought of as _____ on a grand scale.

7. Many of Chicago's more _____ people live in the expensive condominiums on the North Side.

8. Dropping on bended knee, the worshipers _____ before the altar.

9. Ironically, it was from a _____ meeting in the park that the young artist got his first commissions.

10. Over the years the United Fund has become a _____ of people trying to do some good for one another.

11. The _____ bed of the ancient river curled back on itself again and again.

12. The _____ of the Ohio River and the Mississippi River occurs near Cairo, Illinois.

MATCHING

_____ 1. super*flu*ous

_____ 2. af*flu*ent

_____ 3. in*flec*tion

_____ 4. con*flu*ence

_____ 5. genu*flect*

_____ 6. con*fratern*ity

_____ 7. *fratr*icide

_____ 8. *flex*uous

_____ 9. *fratern*ize

_____10. *fort*e

_____11. *fort*uitous

_____12. *fort*itude

_____11. *fort*uitous

_____12. *fort*itude

a. a running or flowing together, as rivers or ideas
b. to mix together (socialize) in a brotherly fashion; to associate with
c. strength of character; patient courage
d. a society (of men) united for a specific purpose
e. flowing with wealth and abundance; prosperous
f. to drop to one knee in a prayer position
g. happening by the chance of good luck; unplanned
h. (flowing) beyond what is needed; needlessly abundant
i. the killing of a brother, or one who commits such an act
j. one's special area of accomplishment
k. a slight change in tone or modulation of the voice; a point of emphasis
l. winding in and out; bending or wavering

SENTENCE COMPLETION

1. All *superfluous* considerations aside, we had _____

_____

2. This *confraternity* of malcontents will _____

_____

3. Why should so much *fortitude* be required to _____

_____

4. A series of *flexuous* designs had been _____

_____

41

5. There was a great *confluence* of unusual ideas at _____

_____

6. The first instance of Biblical *fratricide* involved _____

_____

7. I did not understand the intent of the speaker's strange *inflection* when he _____

_____

8. The young woman claimed that her *forte* was _____

_____

9. For a society as *affluent* as ours, _____

_____

10. I would prefer to *fraternize* with _____

_____

11. The garden's apparently *fortuitous* design _____

_____

12. Dunston's nervous *genuflecting* causes _____

_____

Words from Latin Roots (9)

ROOTS

1. *fus, fund, found* (pour, melt): transfusion, refund, foundry _____

   _____

2. *grad, gress* (go, step, walk): gradual, progress _____

   _____

3. *grat* (please, favor): congratulate _____

4. *greg* (flock, herd, blend): congregation _____

   _____

WORD LIST

1. ag*greg*ation (*ag*-rə-GAY-shən): separate individuals joined in a group, often for a specific purpose
2. con*found* (kən-FAUND): to perplex, confuse, amaze, bewilder
3. de*grad*ation (*deg*-rə-DAY-shən): a major reduction in social status or moral character
4. di*gress* (diy-GRES): to ramble off the point
5. ef*fus*ive (i-FYUW-siv): pouring forth in an emotional way; unrestrained
6. e*greg*ious (i-GREE-jəs): standing out from others, but in a bad way; flagrant
7. e*gress* (EE-gres): an exit; a going out or going forth
8. *grat*uity (grə-TUW-ə-tee): a gift (usually money) given beyond the usual payment
9. *greg*arious (grə-GER-ee-əs): living in flocks or herds; fond of other people
10. in*grat*iate (in-GRAY-shee-*ayt*): to (try to) make oneself appear favorable or necessary to another
11. in*grat*itude (in-GRAT-ə-*tuwd*): a complete absence of gratefulness
12. pro*fus*ion (prə-FYUW-shən): a sort of pouring forth, as of great numbers or abundance

---

a (fat);   ay (fate);   ah (far);   au (doubt);   ch (church);   e (self, care);   ee (evening);   ə (about);   f (flag, phone);   hw (while);   i (fit);   iy (kite);   ŋ (link, sing);   o (audio, corn);   ow (open);   oo (cook);   oi (oil);   sh (shoe, ambition);   th (think);   u (up, love);   uw (ooze);   yu (cure);   yuw (youth, united);   zh (pleasure)

TRUE-FALSE

_____ 1. One is likely to feel a sense of *degradation* at being publicly ridiculed.

_____ 2. It is *ingratitude* that makes us appreciate those who do things for us.

_____ 3. An *egress* is a formal challenge to a duel.

_____ 4. A *gratuity* is given, not purchased.

_____ 5. *Gregarious* individuals are generally sociable.

_____ 6. To *digress* is to stick rigidly to the topic.

_____ 7. *Egregious* behavior is likely to be noticed by other people.

_____ 8. A *profusion* of anything is a chronic shortage.

_____ 9. To *ingratiate* is to make a permanent enemy of.

_____10. *Effusive* individuals are often very emotional.

_____11. An *aggregation* is a type of plastic patio furniture.

_____12. To *confound* is to train for gainful employment.

SENTENCE FILL-IN

1. Such an _____ manner, even in a friend, becomes fatiguing after a time.

2. Excuse me if I _____, but I simply must tell you about my uncle's giraffe.

3. Since old people are allowed little control over their own affairs, aging is often seen as

   a kind of _____.

4. A _____ of wild flowers decorated the forest ballroom.

5. An _____ liar, Logan will say anything that pops into his head, no matter how far afield of the truth.

6. The complexity of a large city can easily _____ one unaccustomed to great numbers of people.

7. The casual _____ of children can sometimes be devastating to their parents.

8. An _____ of angry property owners gathered outside the assessor's office.

9. Our usual Christmas _____ is a very lean and partially frozen turkey.

44

10. Make certain that the deed to the property guarantees you the right of _____ .

11. Why bother to _____ yourself with this fellow when he will be out of office in six months?

12. Preferring to keep to himself, Luther is not a very _____ individual.

MATCHING

_____ 1. pro*fus*ion

_____ 2. ag*greg*ation

_____ 3. in*grat*iate

_____ 4. con*found*

_____ 5. in*grat*itude

_____ 6. de*grad*ation

_____ 7. *greg*arious

_____ 8. di*gress*

_____ 9. *grat*uity

_____10. ef*fus*ive

_____11. e*gress*

_____12. e*greg*ious

a. living in flocks or herds; fond of other people
b. to (try to) make oneself appear favorable or necessary to another
c. standing out from others, but in a bad way; flagrant
d. a major reduction in social status or moral character
e. to perplex, confuse, amaze, bewilder
f. a sort of pouring forth, as of great numbers or abundance
g. an exit; a going out or going forth
h. separate individuals joined in a group, often for a specific purpose
i. pouring forth in an emotional way; unrestrained
j. to ramble off the point
k. a gift (usually money) given beyond the usual payment
l. a complete absence of gratefulness

SENTENCE COMPLETION

1. My cat, an unusually *gregarious* little creature, often _____

_____

2. There seemed a *profusion* of madness among _____

_____

3. Such bitter *ingratitude* doesn't really _____

_____

45

4. A disappointingly small *aggregation* of _____

_____

5. *Ingratiating* oneself to the masses can _____

_____

6. Let us *digress* for a moment to _____

_____

7. We hardly expected such an *effusive* _____

_____

8. The *degradations* of poverty can leave _____

_____

9. These *egregious* plots of yours _____

_____

10. We were again *confounded* by _____

_____

11. Refusing such a small *gratuity*, the waiter _____

_____

12. Our point of *egress* will be _____

_____

Words from Latin Roots (10)

ROOTS

1. *hosp*(*it*), *host* (guest, host):   hospital, hostess _____

2. *jac*(*t*), *ject* (throw, hurl, lie):   reject _____

   _____

3. *jud*(*ic*) (judge, judgment):   judicial _____

4. *junct, join* (join):   junction, disjoint _____

   _____

WORD LIST

1. ad*jac*ent (ə-JAY-sənt):   near, close by, or next to
2. ad*judic*ate (ə-JUW-də-*kayt*):   to settle or rule upon, as in a court of law
3. ad*junct* (AJ-uŋkt):   a thing (of secondary importance) added to something
4. con*ject*ure (kən-JEK-chər):   the formation of a point of view without proof; an inference or guesswork
5. en*join* (in-JOIN):   to urge or order, as with stern authority; to command
6. *host*elry (HAHS-təl-ree):   a place of lodging, as an inn
7. *host*ler (HAHS-lər):   a person who services trucks at the end of a run; one who cares for horses at an inn
8. in*hospit*able (in-HAHS-pi-tə-bəl):   disinclined to be kind or friendly; barren and forbidding
9. in*judic*ious (*in*-juw-DISH-əs):   displaying indiscreet or poor judgment
10. pre*judic*ial (*prej*-ə-DISH-əl):   characteristic of an unfavorable opinion held without supporting evidence
11. re*join*der (ri-JOIN-dər):   a quick and clever answer; an appropriate reply
12. tra*ject*ory (trə-JEK-tə-ree):   the curved path of an object in flight

---

a (fat);   ay (fate);   ah (far);   au (doubt);   ch (church);   e (self, care);   ee (evening);   ə (about);   f (flag, phone);   hw (while);   i (fit);   iy (kite);   ŋ (link, sing);   o (audio, corn);   ow (open);   oo (cook);   oi (oil);   sh (shoe, ambition);   th (think);   u (up, love);   uw (ooze);   yu (cure);   yuw (youth, united);   zh (pleasure)

47

TRUE-FALSE

_____ 1. A *trajectory* is a type of electronic circuit.

_____ 2. Objects *adjacent* to each other are in total isolation from one another.

_____ 3. To *enjoin* someone to do something is to beg on bended knee.

_____ 4. When people are *inhospitable,* it is reasonable to assume that they do not wish to be in our company.

_____ 5. An *injudicious* decision is a wise one.

_____ 6. A modern-day *hostler* should know a good deal about diesel engines.

_____ 7. *Adjunct* personnel usually hold the highest and most important positions in a company.

_____ 8. *Prejudicial* judgments are usually fair and objective.

_____ 9. A *hostelry* can be a pleasant place to spend the night.

_____10. *Conjecture* is generally speculative.

_____11. To *adjudicate* is to ignore successfully.

_____12. An angry *rejoinder* might well embarrass the person to whom it is addressed.

SENTENCE FILL-IN

1. The case was thrown out of court because the judge had allowed the presentation of _____ evidence.

2. The company's regulations _____ all office personnel to be at their work stations by 9:00 A.M.

3. Acme Trucking was forced to close down when the _____ union went on strike.

5. Our host told us that in ages past the _____ had been run by monks.

6. The company's new facility is located _____ to the old one.

7. As an _____ to the main contract, we should seek a performance bond.

8. A missile's _____ depends upon many things, one of which is the force with which the missile is launched.

9. Yes, it was _____ of you to invite your ex-wife to your wedding.

10. In the end the instructor admitted that he had left himself open for Millicent's clever

   _____ .

11. Though _____, the moors of the Scottish Highlands are beautiful and intriguing.

12. Though such _____ is interesting enough, it has no basis in fact.

MATCHING

_____ 1. tra*ject*ory

_____ 2. ad*jac*ent

_____ 3. re*join*der

_____ 4. ad*judic*ate

_____ 5. pre*judic*ial

_____ 6. ad*junct*

_____ 7. in*judic*ious

_____ 8. con*ject*ure

_____ 9. in*hospit*able

_____ 10. en*join*

_____ 11. *host*ler

_____ 12. *host*elry

a. a quick and clever answer; an appropriate reply

b. disinclined to be kind or friendly; barren and forbidding

c. a place for lodging, as an inn

d. the curved path of an object in flight

e. displaying indiscreet or poor judgment

f. to settle or rule upon, as in a court of law

g. to urge or order, as with stern authority; to command

h. a person who services trucks at the end of a run; one who cares for horses at an inn

i. near, close by, or next to

j. characteristic of an unfavorable opinion held without supporting evidence

k. the formation of a point of view without proof; an inference or guesswork

l. a thing (of secondary importance) added to something else

SENTENCE COMPLETION

1. From the old-time *hostler* we rented _____

_____

2. In his position as an *adjunct* director, Boris is responsible for _____

_____

3. As usual, the dean's attempt at a *rejoinder* was _____

_____

4. To get things started, Duncan made his usual *injudicious* remarks about _____

    _____

5. Our guide was an *inhospitable* chap who _____

    _____

6. The vice-president *enjoined* the protesting students to _____

    _____

7. The asteroid's projected *trajectory* made it necessary to _____

    _____

8. Who has the authority to *adjudicate* a case in which _____

    _____

9. To indulge in this sort of *conjecture* is _____

    _____

10. After three nights in a rustic *hostelry,* we decided _____

    _____

11. Many people label as *prejudicial* any opinion they _____

    _____

12. The houses *adjacent* to the stream will be _____

    _____

Words from Latin Roots (11)

ROOTS

1. *jur* (swear):   juror _____

2. *liber, liver* (free):   liberty, delivery _____

3. *liter(a)* (letter):   literacy _____

   _____

4. *loc* (place):   location _____

WORD LIST

1. ab*jure* (ab-JOOR):   to renounce (under oath), as rights or opinions
2. al*litera*tion (ə-*lit*-ə-RAY-shən):   the repetition of the same consonant sound in closely positioned words, as in "Peter Piper picked a peck of pickled peppers"
3. *jur*isdiction (*joor*-əs-DIK-shən):   the area or region of authority
4. *liber*alize (LIB-ər-ə-*liyz*):   to make or become less provincial or narrow
5. *liber*tarian (*lib*-ər-TER-ee-ən):   one who believes in equal civil liberties for everyone; advocating freedom for all
6. *liber*tine (LIB-ər-*teen*):   without moral or sexual restraints; a free-living person
7. *liter*ati (*lit*-ə-RAH-tee):   collectively, the educated members of society
8. *loc*alism (LOW-kə-*liz*-əm):   an expression (manner) typical of a specific region
9. *loc*omotion (*low*-kə-MOW-shən):   the power or action of moving from place to place
10. ob*liter*ate (ə-BLIT-ə-*rayt*):   to destroy all traces of; to obscure completely
11. per*jury* (PUR-jə-ree):   deliberately giving false information under oath
12. re*loc*ate (ree-LOW-*kayt*):   to move to a new place, especially a new residence

---

a (*f*a*t*);   ay (*f*a*te*);   ah (*f*ar);   au (*do*u*bt*);   ch (*ch*ur*ch*);   e (*se*lf, *c*are);   ee (*e*vening);   ə (*a*bout);   f (*f*lag, *ph*one);   hw (*wh*ile);   i (*f*i*t*);   iy (*k*i*te*);   ŋ (li*nk*, si*ng*);   o (*au*dio, *c*orn);   ow (*o*pen);   oo (*c*oo*k*);   oi (*oi*l);   sh (*sh*oe, ambi*ti*on);   th (*th*ink);   u (*u*p, l*o*ve);   uw (*ooze*);   yu (*c*ure);   yuw (*y*outh, *u*nited);   zh (plea*s*ure)

TRUE-FALSE

_____ 1. *Perjury* is usually punishable by death.

_____ 2. One would normally expect a *libertarian* to oppose such things as the Equal Rights Amendment.

_____ 3. An object's source of *locomotion* is what makes it move.

_____ 4. To *abjure* is to support with money.

_____ 5. To *obliterate* a message is to make it more easily read.

_____ 6. A *libertine* is likely to be considered immoral by many people.

_____ 7. Local police have *jurisdiction* only in their own state.

_____ 8. We normally expect the *literati* to be well read.

_____ 9. "You all" is an example of a Southern *localism*.

_____ 10. To *liberalize* is to make stubborn and inflexible.

_____ 11. *Alliteration* is often popular in children's poems.

_____ 12. To *relocate* is to refuse to take nourishment.

SENTENCE FILL-IN

1. The seasons will gradually _____ all that remains of the old village.

2. The old _____ brags that he has had six wives and dozens of mistresses.

3. After admitting having committed _____, Leland was no longer a trusted member of management.

4. Dr. Martin Luther King, Jr., was an influential civil _____ of the 1960s.

5. The visiting lecturer was clearly amused by the overweening self-esteem of the local

   _____.

6. The dean maintains that the city police have no _____ on the campus.

7. You might be well advised to _____ your former position on the matter.

8. To become an accepted member of the free world community, the Soviet Union will have

   to _____ many of its institutions.

9. If I am to take this new position, I must _____ house and home.

52

10. The poet said that _____ was not a device currently used by serious poets.

11. The diesel engine has replaced the steam engine as a source of _____ for train travel.

12. The word "twister" is a Western _____ for a tornado.

MATCHING

_____ 1. per*jury*

_____ 2. re*loc*ate

_____ 3. al*litera*tion

_____ 4. ob*liter*ate

_____ 5. *jur*isdiction

_____ 6. ab*jure*

_____ 7. *loco*motion

_____ 8. *liber*alize

_____ 9. *loc*alism

_____ 10. *liber*tarian

_____ 11. *liter*ati

_____ 12. *liber*tine

a. to destroy all traces of; to obscure completely
b. to renounce (under oath), as rights or opinions
c. the power or action of moving from place to place
d. an expression (manner) typical of a specific region
e. collectively, the educated members of society
f. without moral or sexual restraints; a free-living person
g. to make or become less provincial or narrow
h. the area or region of authority
i. deliberately giving false information under oath
j. one who believes in equal civil liberties for everyone; advocating freedom for all
k. to move to a new place, especially a new residence
l. the repetition of the same consonant sound in closely positioned words, as in "Peter Piper picked a peck of pickled peppers"

SENTENCE COMPLETION

1. To *relocate* an entire village _____

_____

2. These weekend *libertines* don't _____

_____

3. Humorous *alliterations* were used by _____

_____

53

4. Th___ h your *libertarian* sentiments may sound convincing to those who don't know you, I___ e _____

_____

5. ___ccused of *perjury*, James _____

_____

Minnie's speech is always sprinkled with such *localisms* as _____

_____

7. The village *literati* insisted that _____

_____

8. Nuclear *locomotion* is as yet _____

_____

9. In the past few years we have *liberalized* many _____

_____

10. The best time to *abjure* your allegiance to such a candidate is _____

_____

11. Take this acid solution and *obliterate* every _____

_____

12. The U.S. Coast Guard has no *jurisdiction* in _____

_____

Words from Latin Roots (12)

ROOTS

1. *loqu, locut* (speak, talk):   eloquent, elocution _____

_____

2. *luc, lumin* (light, shine):   lucid, illuminate _____

_____

3. *man(u)* (hand):   manicure, manuscript _____

_____

4. *mater(n), matr* (mother):   maternal, matricide _____

_____

WORD LIST

1. circum*locut*ion (*sur*-kəm-low-KYUW-shən):   talking all around a subject without coming to the point
2. col*loqu*ial (kə-LOW-kwee-əl):   related to ordinary, conversational language usage
3. e*luc*idate (i-LUW-sə-*dayt*):   to shed some light on, as through clear explanation
4. e*man*cipate (i-MAN-sə-*payt*):   to set free from bondage
5. *loqu*acious (low-KWAY-shəs):   too talkative; excessively wordy
6. *lumin*ary (LUW-mə-*ner*-ee):   any particularly brilliant, famous, or well-known personality
7. *man*date (MAN-*dayt*):   an authoritative command or popular charge
8. *man*ifesto (*man*-ə-FES-tow):   a formal (public) statement of intentions
9. *matr*iarch (MAY-tree-*ahrk*):   a woman who rules, as in a family or local tribe
10. *matr*iculate (mə-TRIK-yə-*layt*):   to enroll, as in a college or university
11. *matr*ix (MAY-triks):   any type of mold, form, or casting
12. pel*luc*id (pə-LUW-sid):   presented in such a way that understanding is clear and simple; showing maximum clarity

---

a (*f*a*t*); ay (*f*a*te*); ah (*f*a*r*); au (*do*u*bt*); ch (*church*); e (*self, care*); ee (*evening*); ə (*about*); f (*f*lag, *ph*one); hw (*wh*ile); i (*f*i*t*); iy (*k*i*te*); ŋ (li*nk*, si*ng*); o (*au*dio, c*or*n); ow (*o*pen); oo (c*oo*k); oi (*oi*l); sh (*sh*oe, ambi*ti*on); th (*th*ink); u (*u*p, l*o*ve); uw (*ooze*); yu (c*u*re); yuw (*youth, u*nited); zh (plea*s*ure)

55

4. After a dozen years of resistance, the club will *matriculate* _____

_____

5. The speaker's penchant for *colloquial* expressions _____

_____

6. The *pellucid* waters of the secluded lake _____

_____

7. Though a master of bluster and *circumlocution,* Warren seldom _____

_____

8. The *matrix* for these castings was _____

_____

9. We can never completely *emancipate* ourselves from _____

_____

10. The aged *matriarch* continued _____

_____

11. Several *luminaries* from the university visited the _____

_____

12. The terrorists published a *manifesto* in which _____

_____

Words from Latin Roots (13)

ROOTS

1. *medi* (middle):   medium _____

2. *mem(or)* (mindful, remembering):   memorial _____

3. *migr* (wander):   migration _____

4. *mit(t)*, *miss* (send):   transmit, missile _____

_____

WORD LIST

1. com*memor*ate (kə-MEM-ə-*rayt*):   to honor the memory of by some celebration
2. e*migr*ant (EM-ə-grənt):   a person who leaves one country to settle somewhere else
3. e*miss*ary (EM-ə-*ser*-ee):   a person or group sent off on an important mission
4. im*migr*ant (EM-ə-grənt):   one who moves into a region (country) for the first time
5. inter*mitt*ent (*in*-tər-MIT-ənt):   stopping and starting at various intervals
6. *medi*an (MEE-dee-ən):   a midpoint or divider
7. *medi*ate (MEE-dee-*ayt*):   to settle differences (between parties), as by compromise
8. *medi*ocrity (*mee*-dee-AHK-rə-tee):   the condition of being very ordinary
9. *memor*abilia (*mem*-ər-ə-BIL-ee-ə):   a collection of all sorts of (objects) information, as from the past
10. *memor*andum (*mem*-ə-RAN-dəm):   a short note intended to jog the memory
11. *migr*atory (MIY-grə-*tor*-ee):   moving from place to place, especially seasonally
12. pre*mise* (PREM-is):   a basic statement or position from which one develops an argument

---

a (*f*at);   ay (*f*ate);   ah (*f*ar);   au (*d*ou*bt*);   ch (*church*);   e (*self*, *care*);   ee (*evening*);   ə (*about*);   f (*f*lag, *ph*one);   hw (*wh*ile);   i (*f*it);   iy (*k*ite);   ŋ (li*nk*, si*ng*);   o (*au*dio, *corn*);   ow (*open*);   oo (*cook*);   oi (*oil*);   sh (*sh*oe, ambi*t*ion);   th (*th*ink);   u (*up*, *love*);   uw (*ooze*);   yu (*cure*);   yuw (*youth*, *united*);   zh (plea*s*ure)

59

TRUE-FALSE

_____ 1. A government *emissary* can expect to do a good deal of traveling.

_____ 2. A *memorandum* is normally taken with a glass of water to help one forget the day's disappointments.

_____ 3. An *immigrant* is a person who moves out of one country on the way to another.

_____ 4. Program *mediocrity* seems to be the goal of much television entertainment.

_____ 5. A *premise* is a proven fact.

_____ 6. To *mediate* is to make a situation considerably worse.

_____ 7. A memorial funeral service is intended to *commemorate* the life of the deceased.

_____ 8. *Migratory* creatures remain in the same place for a lifetime.

_____ 9. A *median* is a fortune-teller.

_____10. A collection of *memorabilia* will likely bring the past to mind.

_____11. *Intermittent* progress is likely to be uneven.

_____12. An *emigrant* is a person who moves into a new region.

SENTENCE FILL-IN

1. At Christmas, we are supposed to _____ the birth of Christ.

2. Jewish _____ are today flocking out of the Soviet Union.

3. Though the showers were _____, the picnic was called off.

4. Why bother to _____ a quarrel between two outlaw mobs?

5. The president has again sent an _____ to Egypt to try to mend some diplomatic fences.

6. Flocks of _____ birds visit my swamp twice each year.

7. After years of _____, the aging novelist produced a savage and wonderful tale.

8. Members of the campus Vets Club are gathering _____ from World War II.

9. Your conclusion is false for the simple reason that your _____ was false.

10. In the early years of the twentieth century, thousands of _____ from all over Europe came to the United States.

11. Our history instructor said that the _____ score on the examination was 72.

12. Heathcliff is so absentminded that he needs a _____ to remind him where to go to work every morning.

MATCHING

_____ 1. pre*mise*

_____ 2. com*memor*ate

_____ 3. *migr*atory

_____ 4. e*migr*ant

_____ 5. *memor*andum

_____ 6. e*miss*ary

_____ 7. *memor*abilia

_____ 8. im*migr*ant

_____ 9. *medi*ocrity

_____ 10. inter*mitt*ent

_____ 11. *medi*ate

_____ 12. *medi*an

a. one who moves into a region (country) for the first time

b. a short note intended to jog the memory

c. a basic statement or position from which one develops an argument

d. to settle differences (between parties), as by compromise

e. to honor the memory of by some celebration

f. a person who leaves one country to settle somewhere else

g. a person or group sent off on an important mission

h. a midpoint or divider

i. the condition of being very ordinary

j. a collection of all sorts of (objects) information, as from the past

k. moving from place to place, especially seasonally

l. stopping and starting at various intervals

SENTENCE COMPLETION

1. A properly written *memorandum* should include _____

_____

2. *Migratory* bands of Gypsies pass _____

_____

3. *Intermittent* applause throughout the performance made _____

_____

61

4. The only *memorabilia* Ernest has left from twenty years in the Marines are _____

_____

5. These *immigrants* brought with them _____

_____

6. The *median* on interstate highways was originally intended to _____

_____

7. Each year the small community *commemorates* _____

_____

8. As *emissaries* of peace and Christian living, a group of young _____

_____

9. The union requested that we call in an outsider to *mediate* the _____

_____

10. One of the first *emigrants* to leave famine-stricken Ireland, Sharon's grandfather _____

_____

11. Middle-class *mediocrity* is what _____

_____

12. Let's begin with the *premise* that _____

_____

Words from Latin Roots (14)

ROOTS

1. *mod* (measure, manner): modern _____

2. *mor(t)* (death): mortician _____

3. *mov, mot, mob* (move): movable, remote, mobile _____

 _____

4. *nov* (new): novelty _____

WORD LIST

1. a*mort*ize (AM-ər-*tiyz*): to pay off or liquidate, as a debt; to depreciate the value of, as a building or equipment

2. com*mod*ious (kə-MOW-dee-əs): spacious, suitable, and well appointed

3. com*mot*ion (kə-MOW-shən): violent turbulence or noisy and confused rushing about

4. im*mov*ilize (i-MOW-bə-*liyz*): to bring to a halt; to prevent from moving

5. in*nov*ation (in-ə-VAY-shən): something new and different, as a method or process

6. *mod*icum (MAHD-i-kəm): a small amount or portion

7. *mod*ulate (MAHJ-ə-*layt*): to arrange, adjust, or vary—as tone or pitch

8. *mor*ibund (MOR-ə-*bund*): near death, or deathlike; without vitality

9. *mort*ify (MOR-tə-*fiy*): to embarrass publicly; to punish (oneself)

10. *mot*ivation (*mow*-tə-VAY-shən): anything causing a person to act; an inducement

11. *nov*ice (NAHV-is): a person new at any task or activity; a beginner

12. re*nov*ate (REN-ə-*vayt*): to make (appear) new and fresh again; to renew

TRUE-FALSE

_____ 1. An *innovation* sometimes results from looking at old problems in new ways.

_____ 2. We normally think of a *commotion* as a great sleep.

---

a (fat); ay (fate); ah (far); au (doubt); ch (church); e (self, care); ee (evening); ə (about); f (flag, phone); hw (while); i (fit); iy (kite); ŋ (link, sing); o (audio, corn); ow (open); oo (cook); oi (oil); sh (shoe, ambition); th (think); u (up, love); uw (ooze); yu (cure); yuw (youth, united); zh (pleasure)

_____ 3. To *modulate* is to run wild in the streets.

_____ 4. We *renovate* buildings to make them usable again.

_____ 5. To *immobilize* is to bring to a stop.

_____ 6. A *moribund* appearance is vital and healthy looking.

_____ 7. To *mortify* one's parents is to make them very proud.

_____ 8. A *novice* is a person who is experienced at everything.

_____ 9. To *amortize* a debt is to refuse to pay it.

_____10. *Motivation* is what makes us run.

_____11. A *commodious* design is likely to have been made with creature comforts in mind.

_____12. A *modicum* of pleasure, by any measure, is excessive.

SENTENCE FILL-IN

1. An inflated self-image is sometimes the _____ that drives a certain type of person to seek public office.

2. When we left the city and moved to the country, it took us a while to _____ our lives to the slower pace of living.

3. The international oil cartel could easily _____ American industry.

4. Current tax laws allow businesses to _____ large capital expenditures over a relatively short period of time.

5. To everyone's amazement, a _____ won the professional tennis tournament.

6. After three months on the road, Stanley and Ruth found their small apartment quite

   _____ .

7. Waking up stark naked on a city street is enough to _____ most people.

8. Microwave ovens are an expensive and perhaps dangerous _____ for the kitchen.

9. The wounded soldier lay in a _____ state for several days before finally dying.

10. Though Benjamin's story is based on a _____ of truth, it is for the most part a fabrication of his mind.

11. Three young people caused a great _____ by riding horses through the hotel lobby.

12. Our statistics tell us that we can _____ the old structure for less than half what it would cost to put up a new one.

MATCHING

_____ 1. re*nov*ate

_____ 2. a*mort*ize

_____ 3. *nov*ice

_____ 4. com*mod*ious

_____ 5. *mot*ivation

_____ 6. com*mot*ion

_____ 7. *mort*ify

_____ 8. im*mob*ilize

_____ 9. *mor*ibund

_____10. in*nov*ation

_____11. *mod*ulate

_____12. *mod*icum

a. to bring to a halt; to prevent from moving
b. near death, or deathlike; without vitality
c. violent turbulence or noisy and confused rushing about
d. something new and different, as a method or process
e. to make (appear) new and fresh again; to renew
f. a person new at any task or activity; a beginner
g. to pay off or liquidate, as a debt; to depreciate the value of, as a building or equipment
h. spacious, suitable, and well appointed
i. a small amount or portion
j. to arrange, adjust, or vary—as tone or pitch
k. to embarrass publicly; to punish (oneself)
l. anything causing a person to act; an inducement

SENTENCE COMPLETION

1. As members of the local historical society were *renovating* the old jail, they _____

_____

2. Without proper *motivation,* these people will _____

_____

3. Even a *novice* should _____

_____

4. Since we were unable to *modulate* the tone properly, _____

_____

5. *Mortified* by what she was being told, Margot _____

_____

6. Though we have blasted the enemy for three days and nights, we have been unable to

immobilize _____

_____

7. The *moribund* demeanor of the _____

_____

8. I have never seen such a *commotion* as _____

_____

9. A *modicum* of luxury no longer seems _____

_____

_____

10. If we *amortize* the cost of these stamping machines over a period of only a few years, we

_____

_____

11. The *commodious* apartment included _____

_____

12. What was advertised as an *innovation* in _____

_____

Words from Latin Roots (15)

ROOTS

1. *pater(n)*, *patr* (father): paternity, patriot _____

_____

2. *ped* (foot): pedal _____

3. *pend*, *pens* (hang, weigh, pay): pendulum, expense _____

_____

4. *plac* (please): placid _____

WORD LIST

1. ap*pend*age (ə-PEN-dij): anything (of subordinate importance) added to something else
2. com*plac*ent (kəm-PLAY-sənt): passively pleased with oneself; smug and self-satisfied
3. im*ped*iment (im-PED-ə-mənt): something that gets in the way of or entangles
4. im*pend*ing (im-PEN-diŋ): likely to happen at any moment
5. *patern*alism (pə-TUR-nə-*liz*-əm): a controlling of situations, as with a strong fatherly hand
6. *patr*ician (pə-TRISH-ən): (a person) of the higher or ruling class; noble and cultured
7. *patr*on (PAY-trən): one who supports, protects, or encourages another
8. *ped*estrian (pə-DES-tree-ən): very ordinary; without cleverness, interest, or imagination
9. *pens*ive (PEN-siv): deeply or wistfully thoughtful, as if the mind were suspended
10. *plac*ate (PLAY-kayt): to calm another's anger; to appease or pacify
11. *plac*ebo (plə-SEE-bow): a supposed medicine given to patients only to satisfy them
12. sesqui*ped*alian (*ses*-kwə-pə-DAY-lee-ən): long and involved, especially as related to long words or complex thoughts; a long word

---

a (*fat*); ay (*fate*); ah (*far*); au (*doubt*); ch (*church*); e (*self, care*); ee (*evening*); ə (*about*); f (*flag, phone*); hw (*while*); i (*fit*); iy (*kite*); ŋ (*link, sing*); o (*audio, corn*); ow (*open*); oo (*cook*); oi (*oil*); sh (*shoe, ambition*); th (*think*); u (*up, love*); uw (*ooze*); yu (*cure*); yuw (*youth, united*); zh (*pleasure*)

TRUE-FALSE

_____ 1. A *patrician* is a peasant of the lowest order.

_____ 2. An *appendage* is a thing added to something else.

_____ 3. Sometimes only a few kind words are needed to *placate* an angry heart.

_____ 4. *Complacent* people are always eager for change.

_____ 5. *Sesquipedalian* reasoning is likely to be lengthy and complex.

_____ 6. Corporate *paternalism* has always supported the labor movement.

_____ 7. A *pensive* expression is likely to be indecisive.

_____ 8. An *impediment* often slows down progress.

_____ 9. *Pedestrian* ideas are usually fresh and innovative.

_____10. One expects a *patron* to be generous with money.

_____11. An *impending* event is one that may happen at any minute.

_____12. A *placebo* is a small outdoor garden shelter.

SENTENCE FILL-IN

1. The _____ decline of the stock market has many investors worried.

2. You will never _____ the king's rage by offering him money; it is power he wants.

3. A very wealthy man, Langley can afford to be a _____ of the arts.

4. Though it took Ivan several years of hard work, he has now overcome his speech

   _____.

5. The lady's _____ tastes were beyond both my understanding and my pocketbook.

6. Television generally offers a blend of _____ entertainments.

7. Another unprofitable subsidiary is an _____ this corporation can do without.

8. Blatant _____ was once practiced by owners of professional athletic teams.

9. Mr. Quigley always has that _____ look of one who has been too successful too easily.

10. The _____ youth gazed at the painting for a long time and then sighed.

11. The professor's chronic use of such _____ words and expressions confused half the class and amused the rest.

12. The _____ of public acclaim has cured the nagging self-doubt of many a young literary artist.

MATCHING

_____ 1. sesqui*ped*alian

_____ 2. ap*pend*age

_____ 3. *place*bo

_____ 4. com*plac*ent

_____ 5. *plac*ate

_____ 6. im*ped*iment

_____ 7. *pens*ive

_____ 8. im*pend*ing

_____ 9. *ped*estrian

_____ 10. *patern*alism

_____ 11. *patr*on

_____ 12. *patr*ician

a. to calm another's anger; to appease or pacify

b. a supposed medicine given to patients only to satisfy them

c. (a person) of the higher or ruling class; noble and cultured

d. anything (of subordinate importance) added to something else

e. a controlling of situations, as with a strong fatherly hand

f. something that gets in the way of or entangles

g. passively pleased with oneself; smug and self-satisfied

h. long and involved, especially as related to long words or complex thoughts; a long word

i. deeply or wistfully thoughtful, as if the mind were suspended

j. one who supports, protects, or encourages another

k. likely to happen at any moment

l. very ordinary; without cleverness, interest, or imagination

SENTENCE COMPLETION

1. Such a *pedestrian* view of life leaves _____

_____

2. Our appendix is an anatomical *appendage* that _____

_____

3. In recent years, *paternalism* of any type has _____

_____

4. The most *complacent* group of people I have ever met, these smug _____

_____

5. These *pensive* reveries of yours are beginning _____

_____

6. The patients given the *placebo* did _____

_____

7. Save your *sesquipedalians* for _____

_____

8. The youthful artist's *patron* wanted _____

_____

9. We were faced with one *impediment* after another as _____

_____

10. The teacher did her best to *placate* the _____

_____

11. The announcement of the *impending* death of the _____

_____

12. The gentleman's *patrician* appearance suggested _____

_____

Words from Latin Roots (16)

ROOTS

1. *pon, pos(e)* (put, place, set):   opponent, position _____

   _____

2. *port* (carry):   transportation _____

3. *rog* (ask, beg):   arrogance _____

4. *scrib(e), script* (write):   scribble, scripture _____

   _____

WORD LIST

1. a*scribe* (ə-SKRIYB):   to assign credit, as to a cause or source
2. dis*port* (dis-PORT):   to frolic about in an effort to amuse oneself
3. im*position* (*im*-pə-ZISH-ən):   the placing of one thing on another, as a heavy burden on a person
4. inter*rog*ate (in-TER-ə-*gayt*):   to question or examine at length
5. nonde*script* (*nahn*-di-SKRIPT):   hardly worth taking note of; unremarkable
6. *port*folio (port-FOW-lee-*ow*):   a collection of documents on a topic or an individual; a selection of representative works
7. pre*rog*ative (pri-RAHG-ə-tiv):   a peculiar (unique) right or privilege enjoyed by an individual
8. pro*pon*ent (prə-POW-nənt):   one who consistently supports a movement, position, cause
9. rap*port* (rə-POR):   a generally harmonious relationship between (among) people
10. re*pos*itory (ri-PAHZ-ə-*tor*-ee):   a place where things are stored for safekeeping
11. sub*scribe* (səb-SKRIYB):   to make a pledge to buy; to support, as an idea or doctrine
12. sur*rog*ate (SUR-ə-*gayt*):   a substitute, usually of inferior rank or worth

---

a (*f*at);   ay (*fa*te);   ah (*fa*r);   au (*do*ubt);   ch (*ch*ur*ch*);   e (*se*lf, *ca*re);   ee (*e*vening);   ə (*a*bout);   f (*f*lag, *ph*one);   hw (*wh*ile);   i (*fi*t);   iy (*ki*te);   ŋ (li*nk*, si*ng*);   o (*au*dio, c*o*rn);   ow (*o*pen);   oo (c*oo*k);   oi (*oi*l);   sh (*sh*oe, ambi*ti*on);   th (*th*ink);   u (*u*p, l*o*ve);   uw (*oo*ze);   yu (c*u*re);   yuw (*you*th, *u*nited);   zh (plea*s*ure)

TRUE-FALSE

_____ 1. In the world of business and commerce, individuals are sometimes forced to allow themselves to be represented by their *portfolios*.

_____ 2. A *proponent* is one who is supportive of something.

_____ 3. To *subscribe* to an idea is to reject it out of hand.

_____ 4. To *interrogate* is to say vulgar things in a public place.

_____ 5. Bad *rapport* is likely to be characterized by suspicion and some hostility.

_____ 6. An *imposition* is likely to make your day a little lighter.

_____ 7. A *nondescript* personality is unremarkable.

_____ 8. To *ascribe* is to present a case against.

_____ 9. For the formula-fed infant, the baby bottle becomes a *surrogate* breast.

_____ 10. A *repository* is a place where things are dismantled.

_____ 11. To *disport* is to embarrass publicly.

_____ 12. In a democracy, freedom is the *prerogative* of every citizen.

SENTENCE FILL-IN

1. An extreme _____ of individual freedom, Amos refuses to pay his income tax.

2. In the old prefeminist days, it was considered a woman's _____ to change her mind about almost anything.

3. The young artist took a _____ of his sketches to the New York buyer.

4. A library is a _____ for books, not for knowledge.

5. It is impossible to _____ a sane motive for any such crime.

6. My poor kitten has adopted an old slipper as a _____ mother.

7. The usual series of _____ characters showed up to audition for the bit part.

8. Professor Quinn develops a close _____ with almost all her students.

9. My brother-in-law didn't seem to think it was an _____ for him to live with us all winter.

10. Do the police intend to _____ the suspect all night?

11. Few people today _____ to the notion of a natural aristocracy.

12. Kittens sometimes _____ themselves for hours with a ball of twine.

MATCHING

_____ 1. surrogate

_____ 2. ascribe

_____ 3. subscribe

_____ 4. disport

_____ 5. repository

_____ 6. imposition

_____ 7. rapport

_____ 8. interrogate

_____ 9. proponent

_____10. nondescript

_____11. prerogative

_____12. portfolio

a. hardly worth taking note of; unremarkable

b. the placing of one thing on another, as a heavy burden on a person

c. a generally harmonious relationship between (among) people

d. one who consistently supports a movement, position, cause

e. a collection of documents on a topic or an individual; a selection of representative works

f. to assign credit, as to a cause or source

g. to frolic about in an effort to amuse oneself

h. a substitute, usually of inferior rank or worth

i. to make a pledge to buy; to support, as an idea or doctrine

j. to question or examine at length

k. a place where things are stored for safekeeping

l. a peculiar (unique) right or privilege enjoyed by an individual

SENTENCE COMPLETION

1. We must *ascribe* the success of the celebration to _____

_____

2. In a large city, everyone is forced to put up with the daily *impositions* caused by _____

_____

3. It is not the *prerogative* of the president to _____

_____

4. Though we have *interrogated* a dozen witnesses, we _____

_____

5. Each year the local Arts Council asks me to *subscribe* to _____

_____

6. Our *portfolio* on the enemy agent told us _____

_____

7. The university archives serve as a *repository* for _____

_____

8. A group of drunken sailors *disported* themselves up and down the beach until _____

_____

9. As a *surrogate* parent, the government _____

_____

10. An ardent *proponent* of woman's rights, Natalie refuses _____

_____

11. What began as a relationship with pleasant *rapport* ended _____

_____

12. We passed through several *nondescript* little villages before _____

_____

Words from Latin Roots (17)

ROOTS

1. *sign* (sign): signature _____

2. *simil, simul* (like): similar, simultaneous _____

3. *solv, solu* (loosen, free): dissolve, solution _____

_____

4. *spec(t)*, *spic* (look, appear): inspect, specimen _____

_____

WORD LIST

1. ab*solv*e (əb-ZAHLV): to free from; to acquit, as of charges
2. con*sign* (kən-SIYN): to set aside or apart for a specific purpose; to hand over or entrust
3. dis*simil*ar (di-SIM-ə-lər): not alike; clearly different from
4. dis*solu*tion (*dis*-ə-LUW-shən): a general breakdown or coming apart at the seams
5. fac*simil*e (fak-SIM-ə-lee): a very close copy of, as a document or an edition of a book
6. in*solv*ent (in-SAHL-vənt): unable to meet one's financial responsibilities; broke
7. pro*spect*us (prə-SPEK-təs): a printed program or outline, as of a commercial venture
8. *sign*atory (SIG-nə-*tor*-ee): one who attaches his or her name to a document
9. *sign*et (SIG-nit): an official seal, as for documents or contracts
10. *simul*ate (SIM-yə-*layt*): to make an outward appearance of; to pretend
11. *spec*ious (SPEE-shəs): appearing reasonable, correct, or logical at first glance, but later proving false; not genuine
12. *spec*ulate (SPEK-yə-*layt*): to think about (try to view) various aspects of a subject; to take a chance

---

a (f*a*t); ay (f*a*te); ah (f*a*r); au (d*ou*bt); ch (*ch*ur*ch*); e (s*e*lf, c*a*re); ee (*e*vening); ə (*a*bout); f (*f*lag, *ph*one); hw (*wh*ile); i (f*i*t); iy (k*i*te); ŋ (li*n*k, si*ng*); o (*a*udio, c*o*rn); ow (*o*pen); oo (c*oo*k); oi (*oi*l); sh (*sh*oe, ambi*ti*on); th (*th*ink); u (*u*p, l*o*ve); uw (*oo*ze); yu (c*u*re); yuw (*you*th, *u*nited); zh (pl*e*asure)

75

TRUE-FALSE

_____ 1. A *signatory* is a person who wants to remain anonymous.

_____ 2. To *consign* to oblivion is to remove from the public eye.

_____ 3. A business *prospectus* can be a kind of low-keyed advertisement.

_____ 4. To *simulate* is to confuse one thing with another very much like it.

_____ 5. When the king calls for the *dissolution* of parliament, the session comes to an end.

_____ 6. A *facsimile* looks very much like the real thing.

_____ 7. To *speculate* is to guarantee against economic loss.

_____ 8. To *absolve* is to reduce to a very low temperature.

_____ 9. Royal *signets* were once stamped in hot wax on documents.

_____10. *Specious* arguments must be reasonable to the last detail.

_____11. An *insolvent* organization may find it difficult to borrow money.

_____12. *Dissimilar* sets of circumstances are almost identical.

SENTENCE FILL-IN

1. Let's use the top of the Ping-Pong table to _____ a battlefield.

2. The captain has suggested that we _____ an additional half-dozen teams to the investigation.

3. Though confession may make you feel better, it will not _____ you of the guilt for so heinous a crime.

4. One look at the _____ for the convention told us that we did not care to attend.

5. Cash-flow problems, as well as management's inability to perceive the structure of the current market, have left the company _____.

6. The article went on to say that every member of upper management in both companies was _____ to the agreement.

7. Really, it is illogical to try to compare two such _____ incidents.

8. Your argument is so _____ that it will fool only the most naive.

9. The _____ of the Roman Empire did not occur overnight.

10. Banners displaying the king's _____ preceded the royal procession.

11. I could not believe that Ralph paid $75 for a _____ edition of Mark Twain's *Huckleberry Finn*.

12. It is risky for a person of moderate income to _____ on the stock market.

MATCHING

_____ 1. *spec*ulate

_____ 2. ab*solve*

_____ 3. *spec*ious

_____ 4. con*sign*

_____ 5. *simul*ate

_____ 6. dis*simil*ar

_____ 7. *sign*et

_____ 8. dis*solut*ion

_____ 9. *sign*atory

_____ 10. fac*simile*

_____ 11. pro*spect*us

_____ 12. in*solv*ent

a. appearing reasonable, correct, or logical at first glance, but later proving false; not genuine

b. an official seal, as for documents or contracts

c. a printed program or outline, as of a commercial venture

d. a very close copy of, as a document or an edition of a book

e. not alike; clearly different from

f. to free from; to acquit, as of charges

g. to set aside or apart for a specific purpose; to hand over or entrust

h. a general breakdown or coming apart at the seams

i. unable to meet one's financial responsibilities; broke

j. one who attaches his or her name to a document

k. to make an outward appearance of; to pretend

l. to think about (try to view) various aspects of a subject; to take a chance

SENTENCE COMPLETION

1. A brilliantly colored *signet* _____

_____

2. Though from *dissimilar* backgrounds, the couple _____

_____

3. That so *specious* a proposal could sound _____

_____

4. New evidence *absolved* the accused of _____

_____

5. It's a little late in the game to *speculate* about _____

_____

6. In role-playing exercises, we try to *simulate* how _____

_____

7. Only one of the *signatories* to the original treaty _____

_____

8. Although temporarily *insolvent*, _____

_____

9. The *prospectus* for the new stock issue outlined _____

_____

10. More than a sloppy *facsimile* of the original painting will be needed to _____

_____

11. *Consigned* to jail for his misdeeds, Aldous _____

_____

12. The *dissolution* of the giant corporation began as the result of _____

_____

Words from Latin Roots (18)

ROOTS

1. *tain, ten(t), tinu* (hold):   retain, tenant, continuation _____

_____

2. *tempor* (time):   temporary _____

3. *terr(a)* (earth):   territory _____

4. *test* (to bear witness):   testify _____

WORD LIST

1. abs*tain* (əb-STAYN):   to refrain voluntarily from doing something
2. at*test* (ə-TEST):   to declare (swear) to be true or genuine
3. con*tempor*ary (kən-TEM-pə-*rer*-ee):   present (alive) at the same time; modern
4. de*test* (di-TEST):   to dislike intensely; to hate
5. disin*ter* (*dis*-in-TUR):   to bring back from the grave; to revive or exhume
6. ex*tempor*aneous (ik-*stem*-pə-RAY-nee-əs):   performed with little or no preparation
7. re*tent*ive (ri-TEN-tiv):   holding onto; remembering
8. *tempor*al (TEM-pər-əl):   related to the physical world and thus lasting only a relatively short time
9. *terra* firma (TER-ə-FUR-mə):   the earth viewed as solid and firm
10. *terr*arium (tə-RER-ee-əm):   a glass enclosure containing a garden of small plants
11. *test*imonial (*tes*-tə-MOW-nee-əl):   a statement describing a person's merits and qualifications in a favorable way
12. un*ten*able (un-TEN-ə-bəl):   that which cannot be (logically) held, defended, or maintained.

---

a (*fat*);   ay (*fate*);   ah (*far*);   au (*doubt*);   ch (*church*);   e (*self, care*);   ee (*evening*);   ə (*about*);   f (*flag, phone*);   hw (*while*);   i (*fit*);   iy (*kite*);   ŋ (*link, sing*);   o (*audio, corn*);   ow (*open*);   oo (*cook*);   oi (*oil*);   sh (*shoe, ambition*);   th (*think*);   u (*up, love*);   uw (*ooze*);   yu (*cure*);   yuw (*youth, united*);   zh (*pleasure*)

TRUE-FALSE

_____ 1. The purpose of a *testimonial* is usually character assassination.

_____ 2. A *terrarium* is a large water cooler.

_____ 3. Events that are *contemporary* with each other are from the same time period.

_____ 4. *Terra firma* is the solid earth itself.

_____ 5. To *disinter* is to put to rest permanently.

_____ 6. It is difficult to argue convincingly from an *untenable* point of view.

_____ 7. To *abstain* from drinking alcohol is to overindulge.

_____ 8. An *extemporaneous* speech is carefully prepared in advance.

_____ 9. It isn't unusual for jealous people to *detest* one another.

_____10. A *retentive* mind is unable to remember anything.

_____11. You should *attest* only to what you are certain of.

_____12. *Temporal* creatures can be expected to live indefinitely.

SENTENCE FILL-IN

1. After working for several years as a traveling salesman, I have come to

   _____ the very thought of staying in a motel.

2. At the _____ dinner, I learned what an important man my father was to the community.

3. Perhaps it is time to _____ a few old notions such as each of us being responsible for our own actions.

4. How nice it would be if everyone would _____ from saying negative things about other people.

5. After spending six months in space, I was happy to place my feet on _____.

6. Genghis Khan and Napoleon were not _____ personalities.

7. Having taught for more than twenty years, I can _____ that students have changed in many ways—some good, some not so good.

8. The preacher cautioned his congregation not to concern themselves exclusively with

   _____ pleasures.

80

9. Though it is winter outside, a mini-springtime exists in my _____.

10. This new book on memory development promises to improve the reader's _____ powers by 50 percent.

11. Professor Truman's _____ responses to such difficult questions always amaze me.

12. The bill is politically _____ because it will cost too many votes.

MATCHING

_____ 1. un*ten*able

_____ 2. abs*tain*

_____ 3. *test*imonial

_____ 4. at*test*

_____ 5. *terr*arium

_____ 6. con*tempor*ary

_____ 7. *terra* firma

_____ 8. de*test*

_____ 9. *tempor*al

_____ 10. disin*ter*

_____ 11. re*tent*ive

_____ 12. ex*tempor*aneous

a. to declare (swear) to be true and genuine
b. present (alive) at the same time; modern
c. to bring back from the grave; to revive or exhume
d. holding onto; remembering
e. the earth viewed as solid and firm
f. statements describing a person's merits and qualifications in a favorable way
g. that which cannot be (logically) held, defended, or maintained
h. to refrain voluntarily from doing something
i. to dislike intensely; to hate
j. performed with little or no preparation
k. related to the physical world and thus lasting only a relatively short time
l. a glass enclosure containing a garden of small plants

SENTENCE COMPLETION

1. Our first *extemporaneous* writing assignment came _____

_____

2. The fort is *untenable* because _____

_____

3. Miles and miles of scorched *terra firma* stretched _____

_____

81

4. The *temporal* fads of one age seldom _____

_____

5. Your *retention* of what you read might be better if you _____

_____

6. The very first witness *attested* to _____

_____

7. Evelyn's *contemporary* manner sometimes _____

_____

8. The *testimonial* began with _____

_____

9. My sister's *terrarium* contains _____

_____

10. Perhaps we should all *abstain* from _____

_____

11. These two characters have *detested* each other ever since _____

_____

12. *Disinterred* by the torrential rains, the bodies _____

_____

Words from Latin Roots (19)

ROOTS

1. *tort* (turn, twist): distortion _____

2. *tract* (draw, pull): traction _____

3. *urb* (city): suburban _____

4. *ven*(e), *vent* (come, go): adventure, convenient _____

_____

WORD LIST

1. con*tort*ion (kən-TOR-shən):   the state of being twisted into an unusual shape or position
2. con*ven*e (kən-VEEN):   to assemble for a general (common) purpose
3. con*vent*ional (kən-VEN-shə-nəl):   within the usual or ordinary standards of the day
4. ex*tort*ion (ik-STOR-shən):   getting money by any illegal means
5. inter*urb*an (*in*-tər-UR-bən):   located between two large cities or towns
6. inter*ven*e (*in*-tər-VEEN):   to come or take place between, as between persons or events
7. in*tract*able (in-TRAK-tə-bəl):   very difficult to manage or keep in line; unruly
8. pro*tract*ed (prow-TRAK-tid):   drawn out over a period of time, usually unnecessarily so
9. re*tract* (ri-TRAKT):   to withdraw, as a promise; to take back
10. *tort*uous (TOR-chuw-əs):   characterized by much bending and twisting; devious
11. *urb*anity (ur-BAN-ə-tee):   the mix of qualities suggesting citified civility
12. *urb*anize (UR-bə-*niyz*):   to change (as an area) from rural to citified

TRUE-FALSE

_____ 1. A *protracted* discussion is a short-lived one.

_____ 2. To *urbanize* is to transform into a city.

_____ 3. To *convene* is to dismiss as trivial.

---

a (f*a*t);   ay (f*a*te);   ah (f*a*r);   au (d*ou*bt);   ch (*ch*ur*ch*);   e (s*e*lf, c*a*re);   ee (*e*v*e*ning);   ə (*a*bout);   f (*f*lag, *ph*one);   hw (*wh*ile);   i (f*i*t);   iy (k*i*te);   ŋ (li*n*k, si*ng*);   o (*a*udio, c*o*rn);   ow (*o*pen);   oo (c*oo*k);   oi (*oi*l);   sh (*sh*oe, ambi*ti*on);   th (*th*ink);   u (*u*p, l*o*ve);   uw (*oo*ze);   yu (c*u*re);   yuw (*y*outh, *u*nited);   zh (plea*s*ure)

_____ 4. There were once *interurban* streetcar lines throughout the country.

_____ 5. Anything *conventional* is typical of the standards of the day.

_____ 6. To *retract* what you have said is to repeat it with greater emphasis.

_____ 7. The chief purpose of a *contortion* is to straighten matters out.

_____ 8. A *tortuous* explanation is likely to be clear and direct.

_____ 9. *Intractable* animals are easily trained.

_____ 10. One normally expects a country bumpkin to possess a high degree of *urbanity*.

_____ 11. To *intervene* in someone's affairs is to make those affairs a matter of public record.

_____ 12. *Extortion* is not unusual in a land where people worship money.

SENTENCE FILL-IN

1. Why should I be forced to _____ the charges against the dean when they are true?

2. The speaker's forced _____ was displeasing to the local audience.

3. _____ behavior today includes a broader range of life styles than it did a generation ago.

4. The profit margin on such items as these is so large that it borders on _____.

5. The board members have voted to _____ at nine o'clock sharp.

6. I have to take the _____ bus to get home.

7. My back was twisted all out of shape as a result of the _____ drive through the mountains.

8. Most people would agree that parents have a right to _____ in their children's activities.

9. _____ children are very difficult to teach.

10. Even when he sleeps, my cat is a master of _____.

11. If we _____ the whole world, there will be no place for the wild animals to live.

12. These _____ negotiations between the faculty and the administration could go on forever.

MATCHING

_____ 1. *urb*anize

_____ 2. con*tort*ion

_____ 3. *urb*anity

_____ 4. con*ven*e

_____ 5. *tort*uous

_____ 6. con*ven*tional

_____ 7. re*tract*

_____ 8. ex*tort*ion

_____ 9. pro*tract*ed

_____ 10. inter*urb*an

_____ 11. in*tract*able

_____ 12. inter*ven*e

a. the mix of qualities suggesting citified civility
b. to withdraw, as a promise; to take back
c. to assemble for a general (common) purpose
d. getting money by any illegal means
e. very difficult to manage or keep in line; unruly
f. located between two large cities or towns
g. to come or take place between, as between persons or events
h. to change (as an area) from rural to citified
i. characterized by much bending and twisting; devious
j. drawn out over a period of time, usually unnecessarily so
k. within the usual or ordinary standards of the day
l. the state of being twisted into an unusual shape or position

SENTENCE COMPLETION

1. These *tortuous* exercises in logic will _____

_____

2. Perhaps *interurban* councils are needed to _____

_____

3. An *intractable* collection of prisoners _____

_____

4. Although Mildred dresses in a *conventional* manner, she _____

_____

5. Your verbal *contortions* only _____

_____

6. After a *protracted* investigation, we learned _____

_____

7. As the region has become *urbanized*, _____

_____

8. Though the senator *retracted* his earlier statement, he _____

_____

9. Again accused of *extortion*, the confidence man _____

_____

10. What passes for *urbanity* among _____

_____

11. It is not the government's business to *intervene* in _____

_____

12. We should not *convene* until _____

_____

Words from Latin Roots (20)

ROOTS

1. *vert, vers* (turn): convert, adversary _____

2. *vid, vis* (see): video, visible _____

3. *vit, viv* (life, live): vitamin, vivid _____

4. *voc(at), vok(e)* (call, voice): vocal, vocation, provoke _____

WORD LIST

1. con*vers*ant (kən-VUR-sənt): very familiar with, usually as a result of lengthy experience

2. con*voc*ation (*kahn*-və-KAY-shən): a gathering of a group of people for a specific purpose

3. equi*voc*al (i-KWIV-ə-kəl): that which is misleading because of more than one possible meaning; doubtful or uncertain

4. impro*vise* (IM-prə-*viyz*): to perform without previous preparation

5. in*vid*ious (in-VID-ee-əs): intended to arouse envy, especially through observation

6. in*voke* (in-VOWK): to call upon for help, as a god or devil

7. per*vert*ed (pər-VUR-tid): turned away from that which is considered good, right, and proper

8. re*vit*alize (ree-VIYT-əl-*iyz*): to bring back to life; to put new life into

9. sub*vers*ive (səb-VUR-siv): inclined to overthrow or destroy established institutions

10. *vis*ionary (VIZH-ə-*ner*-ee): one whose head is filled with impractical ideas; with perceptions of the future

11. *viv*acity (vi-VAS-ə-tee): liveliness or animation of disposition

12. *viv*isection (*viv*-ə-SEK-shən): to open for study, as a living or functioning process or system

---

a (fat); ay (fate); ah (far); au (doubt); ch (church); e (self, care); ee (evening); ə (about); f (flag, phone); hw (while); i (fit); iy (kite); ŋ (link, sing); o (audio, corn); ow (open); oo (cook); oi (oil); sh (shoe, ambition); th (think); u (up, love); uw (ooze); yu (cure); yuw (youth, united); zh (pleasure)

TRUE-FALSE

_____ 1. *Demography* is important in the determination of the nation's population.

_____ 2. A *cyclorama* is a vehicle with two large wheels and square pedals.

_____ 3. An *anachronism* is an incident properly described at its actual place in a time sequence.

_____ 4. A *demagogue* is likely to tell the people whatever he thinks will keep him in a position of leadership.

_____ 5. A *cosmopolitan* view of life is likely to be a very narrow view.

_____ 6. An *encyclical* is a general reference volume for the home.

_____ 7. All *pachyderms* have long trunks.

_____ 8. To *synchronize* is to adjust the color pattern so that it will have no clashing hues.

_____ 9. A *cosmonaut* is a bus driver in a large urban area.

_____10. Any *chronological* order is based primarily on space rather than time.

_____11. A *dermatologist* is a logical person to treat a case of acne.

_____12. *Endemic* characteristics are extensive ones, though limited to a definable region or group.

SENTENCE FILL-IN

1. At Gettysburg there is a _____ that depicts the famous Civil War battle that took place there in 1863.

2. Hitler was probably the most sinister _____ of this century.

3. A thorough _____, Henry has lived all over the world.

4. You shouldn't have expected the old _____ to listen to you; he never listens to anyone.

5. Basic history courses are often taught in _____ order.

6. Violence and distrust seem _____ to modern American life.

7. The Bureau of the Census regularly trains people in the art and science of

   _____.

8. Edmund's insistence on wearing such old-fashioned clothes makes him look like a living

   _____.

98

9. I don't seem to be able to _____ my work habits with the rising and setting of the sun.

10. The dean's posted _____ dealing with the litter of empty beer cans soon became a campus joke.

11. There is an opening for a _____ at the university burn center.

12. As far as I know, a Russian _____ has not yet gone to the moon.

MATCHING

_____ 1. syn*chron*ize

_____ 2. ana*chron*ism

_____ 3. pachy*derm*

_____ 4. *chrono*logical

_____ 5. en*dem*ic

_____ 6. *cosmo*naut

_____ 7. en*cycl*ical

_____ 8. *cosmo*politan

_____ 9. *derm*atologist

_____ 10. *cyclo*rama

_____ 11. *demo*graphy

_____ 12. *dem*agogue

a. a circular room with murals painted all around the walls

b. (related to) a letter intended for broad general circulation

c. the representation of anything out of its place in time

d. a physician specializing in diseases of the skin

e. to bring into agreement in terms of time, rate, speed, and so forth

f. one who is too thick-skinned to respond to criticism; an elephant or a rhinoceros

g. possessing the social polish of a person with world-wide experience

h. one who will try anything in order to lead the people

i. peculiar to a specific region or people

j. a person who pilots rocket ships through space

k. arranged in a time sequence or by order of occurrence

l. the science treating such things as population density and distribution, vital statistics, and the like

SENTENCE COMPLETION

1. The woman *cosmonaut* _____

_____

2. The science of *dermatology* _____

_____

3. We were surprised that the *cyclorama* didn't _____

_____

4. The *demographic* survey revealed that _____

_____

5. The novel's first *anachronism* involved _____

_____

6. The insensitive *pachyderm* ignored _____

_____

7. This would-be *demagogue* maintains _____

_____

8. A more careful *chronological* retelling of _____

_____

9. *Synchronize* your watches when _____

_____

10. Visiting large *cosmopolitan* areas can _____

_____

11. Jealousy of one sort or another seems *endemic* to _____

_____

12. The governor's published *encyclical* stated that _____

_____

Words from Greek Roots (3)

ROOTS

1. *dog, dox* (teaching, opinion): dogma, doxology _____

   _____

2. *dyn* (power): dynamite _____

3. *erg, urg* (work): energy, dramaturgy _____

4. *gam* (marriage): bigamy _____

5. *gnos* (know): gnostic _____

WORD LIST

1. a*gnos*tic (ag-NAHS-tik): one who believes that man cannot really know the nature of God

2. *dog*matic (dog-MAT-ik): controlled by a single teaching or doctrine; stated without sufficient proof

3. *dyn*amic (diy-NAM-ik): having power and physical energy; vigorous

4. *dyn*asty (DIY-nəs-tee): the succession of power, as political or family rulers

5. *ergo*nomics (*ur*-gə-NAHM-iks): the science dealing with the adjustment of working conditions to suit the laborers

6. metall*urg*y (MET-əl-*ur*-jee): the science (technology) of removing metal from ores

7. miso*gam*ist (mi-SAHG-ə-məst): one with an intense dislike of the marriage relationship

8. mono*gam*ous (mə-NAHG-ə-məs): related to the practice of being married to one person at a time

9. ortho*dox* (OR-thə-*dahks*): conforming to the "proper" beliefs and customs

10. para*dox*ical (*par*-ə-DAHK-si-kəl): possessing (apparently) contradictory elements

11. pro*gnos*is (prahg-NOW-sis): a forecast, as the outcome of a disease

12. syn*erg*etic (*sin*-ər-JET-ik): working together in a cooperative manner

---

a (fat);   ay (fate);   ah (far);   au (doubt);   ch (church);   e (self, care);   ee (evening);   ə (about);   f (flag, phone);   hw (while);   i (fit);   iy (kite);   ŋ (link, sing);   o (audio, corn);   ow (open);   oo (cook);   oi (oil);   sh (shoe, ambition);   th (think);   u (up, love);   uw (ooze);   yu (cure);   yuw (youth, united);   zh (pleasure)

TRUE-FALSE

_____ 1. An elaborate evening meal may be correctly thought of as a *dynasty*.

_____ 2. Primitive *metallurgy* was sometimes closely associated with magic.

_____ 3. There are no harems in *monogamous* marriages.

_____ 4. An *agnostic* is likely to believe in many gods.

_____ 5. *Dynamic* leaders are usually very vigorous people.

_____ 6. Cooperation is the keystone of any *synergetic* enterprise.

_____ 7. *Ergonomics* is the science dealing with electrical energy.

_____ 8. *Orthodox* tenets are held to be right and proper by those who believe them.

_____ 9. *Dogmatic* individuals can be very stubborn from time to time.

_____10. A true *misogamist* is likely to have several wives at once.

_____11. A physician makes a medical *prognosis* after the death of the patient.

_____12. *Paradoxical* statements often possess a hint of irony.

SENTENCE FILL-IN

1. The students were more than a little surprised to learn that their religion instructor

   was an _____.

2. _____ speakers can move an audience by the power of their words.

3. Though _____ marriages may seem natural to us, other cultures have practiced other types of marriage.

4. Some knowledge of _____ will be needed to melt these coins down.

5. A _____ effort by the whole community was needed to recover from the massive damage done by the flood.

6. How _____ it seems that we spend all our lives working hard in an effort to make it possible not to work at all.

7. A course in _____ falls under the business management umbrella.

8. Ultimately, Leonard's _____ refusal to listen to reason alienated many of his old friends.

9. As it turned out, the doctor's _____ of the patient's chances for recovery could not have been further from the truth.

10. As long as American capitalism survives, so will the Rockefeller _____.

11. An _____ Republican, Mr. Lord believes in the sanctity of the free enterprise system.

12. One wonders how such a thoroughgoing _____ ever came to be married in the first place.

MATCHING

_____ 1. syn*erg*etic

_____ 2. *dog*matic

_____ 3. pro*gnos*is

_____ 4. *dyn*amic

_____ 5. para*dox*ical

_____ 6. *dyn*asty

_____ 7. ortho*dox*

_____ 8. *ergo*nomics

_____ 9. mono*gam*ous

_____ 10. a*gnos*tic

_____ 11. miso*gam*ist

_____ 12. metall*urg*y

a. one who believes that man cannot really know the nature of God

b. conforming to the "proper" beliefs and customs

c. the science (technology) of removing metal from ores

d. working together in a cooperative manner

e. controlled by a single teaching or doctrine; stated without sufficient proof

f. having power and physical energy; vigorous

g. one with an intense dislike of the marriage relationship

h. a forecast, as the outcome of a disease

i. the succession of power, as political or family rulers

j. related to the practice of being married to one person at a time

k. possessing (apparently) contradictory elements

l. the science dealing with the adjustment of working conditions to suit the laborers

SENTENCE COMPLETION

1. Whether *monogamous* by nature or not, _____

_____

2. People are often *dogmatic* when it comes to _____

_____

3. The first *prognosis* suggested that _____

_____

103

4. For an *agnostic*, Charles certainly _____

   _____

5. A lifelong *misogamist*, Andrew _____

   _____

6. Under the American political system, governmental *dynasties* are _____

   _____

7. Somewhat less than *orthodox* in her religious beliefs, Theresa _____

   _____

8. We are searching for a *dynamic* department head to _____

   _____

9. I thought it *paradoxical* that _____

   _____

10. Advances in *metallurgy* have _____

    _____

11. *Synergetic* programs in local neighborhoods can result in _____

    _____

12. *Ergonomical* considerations are today important items in _____

    _____

Words from Greek Roots (4)

ROOTS

1. *gram, graph* (write):   diagram, graphite _____

   _____

2. *hema, hemo, em* (blood):   hemorrhage, leukemia _____

   _____

3. *hydr* (water):   hydrophobia _____

4. *iatr* (medicine, healing):   psychiatrist _____

5. *lith* (stone):   neolithic _____

WORD LIST

1. calli*graph*y (kə-LIG-rə-fee):   the art of beautiful handwriting
2. de*hydr*ated (dee-HIY-dray-tid):   having had all the water removed
3. ger*iatr*ics (*jer*-ee-A-triks):   the branch of medicine treating the diseases of old age
4. *hema*toma (*hee*-mə-TOW-mə):   a blood-filled tumor
5. *hemo*philia (*hee*-mə-FIL-ee-ə):   a condition in which the blood does not clot
6. *hydr*aulic (hiy-DRO-lik):   operated by the movement and force of fluid
7. lexico*graph*er (*lek*-sə-KAHG-rə-fər):   a person who compiles or writes dictionaries
8. *litho*graph (LITH-ə-*graf*):   an artistic print produced on a stone or plate
9. mono*gram* (MAHN-ə-*gram*):   a character combining two or more letters into a single design
10. mono*lith*ic (*mahn*-ə-LITH-ik):   large and as unified and unyielding as a great stone
11. pod*iatr*ist (pow-DIY-ə-trist):   one who specializes in the treatment and prevention of minor foot ailments
12. tox*em*ia (tahk-SEE-mee-ə):   a condition characterized by poisons in the bloodstream

---

a (*f*a*t*); ay (*f*a*t*e); ah (*f*a*r*); au (*do*u*bt*); ch (*ch*ur*ch*); e (*s*e*lf, c*a*re*); ee (*ev*e*ning*); ə (*a*bou*t*); f (*f*lag, *ph*one); hw (*wh*ile); i (*f*i*t*); iy (*k*i*te*); ŋ (li*nk*, si*ng*); o (*au*dio, *c*o*rn*); ow (*o*pen); oo (*c*oo*k*); oi (*oi*l); sh (*sh*oe, ambi*ti*on); th (*th*ink); u (*u*p, l*o*ve); uw (*ooze*); yu (*c*u*re*); yuw (*y*outh, *u*nited); zh (plea*s*ure)

TRUE-FALSE

_____ 1. Ordinary three-speed bicycles have *hydraulic* brakes.

_____ 2. A *hematoma* is a water-filled bruise.

_____ 3. A *lexicographer* should be a real expert on words.

_____ 4. A letter carrier would do well to have a *podiatrist* for a friend.

_____ 5. *Dehydrated* substances are filled with water.

_____ 6. People who suffer from *hemophilia* are sometimes called bleeders.

_____ 7. *Geriatrics* is the branch of veterinary medicine specializing in the treatment of household pets.

_____ 8. A *monogram* can be used for the purpose of identification.

_____ 9. *Calligraphy* involves the engraving of elaborate pictures on stone plates.

_____10. *Toxemia* is a condition characterized by excessive oxygen in the bloodstream.

_____11. A *monolithic* organization is likely to have little room for dissent.

_____12. A *lithograph* is the same thing as an original oil painting.

SENTENCE FILL-IN

1. As the average age of the American citizen increases, _____ becomes a more important branch of medicine.

2. Hamilton's foot became so infected that he was forced to consult a _____.

3. The doctor said that the _____ was originally caused by a severe blow.

4. The communist bloc isn't the _____ structure we once thought it was.

5. Bertram maintains that _____ may result from frequent consumption of chemically treated foods.

6. The typewriter has helped make a lost art of _____.

7. Noah Webster was America's first great _____.

8. Various types of _____ foods are popular among camping enthusiasts.

9. This egotistical character even has his _____ on his shorts.

10. _____ is a blood trait that often runs in families.

11. At the local art festival I bought an original _____ by Bruce McCombs.

12. The water pressure was too low for the _____ press to function well.

MATCHING

_____ 1. tox*em*ia

_____ 2. calli*graph*y

_____ 3. pod*iatr*ist

_____ 4. de*hydr*ated

_____ 5. mono*lith*ic

_____ 6. ger*iatr*ics

_____ 7. mono*gram*

_____ 8. *hema*toma

_____ 9. *litho*graph

_____10. *hemo*philia

_____11. lexico*graph*er

_____12. *hydr*aulic

a. operated by the movement and force of fluid
b. having had all the water removed
c. an artistic print produced on a stone or plate
d. large and as unified and unyielding as a great stone
e. a condition characterized by poisons in the blood-stream
f. the art of beautiful handwriting
g. a condition in which the blood does not clot
h. a person who compiles or writes dictionaries
i. the branch of medicine treating the diseases of old age
j. a character combining two or more letters into a single design
k. one who specializes in the treatment and prevention of minor foot ailments
l. a blood-filled tumor

SENTENCE COMPLETION

1. A *lexicographer's* holiday might consist of _____

_____

2. Persons with *hemophilia* must take care not to _____

_____

3. A sudden failure in the *hydraulic* system caused _____

_____

4. *Dehydrated* by the sun and _____

_____

5. A case of severe *toxemia* caused _____

_____

6. At the national *podiatrists'* convention, _____

_____

7. A specialist in *geriatrics,* Dr. Johnson _____

_____

8. The *monolithic* proportions of _____

_____

9. The *hematoma* was a direct result of _____

_____

10. *Monogrammed* silverware seems to me a _____

_____

11. During the Middle Ages, *calligraphy* often rose to _____

_____

12. Muriel's collection of *lithographs* includes _____

_____

Words from Greek Roots (5)

ROOTS

1. *log(ue)* (word, speech, study): logical, travelogue _____

_____

2. *meter, metr* (measure): barometer, metric _____

_____

3. *morph* (form, shape): morphology _____

4. *neur* (nerve): neuron _____

5. *nom* (rule, law, order): economics _____

WORD LIST

1. agro*nom*ist (ə-GRAHN-ə-mist): an expert in the entire business of growing crops and managing a large farm
2. a*morph*ous (ə-MOR-fəs): with little observable shape or form
3. asym*metr*ical (*as*-ə-ME-trə-kəl): lacking balance of form or proportion
4. gastro*nom*y (gas-TRAHN-ə-mee): the delicate art of knowing about and enjoying good food
5. *log*orrhea (lo-gə-REE-ə): an excessive flow of words; talkativeness
6. meta*morph*osis (*met*-ə-MOR-fə-sis): a gradual but complete transformation
7. *metr*onome (ME-trə-*nowm*): a pendulum device that beats out (musical) tempo
8. neo*log*ism (nee-AHL-ə-*jiz*-əm): a new word or an old word used in a new way
9. *neur*itis (noo-RIY-təs): inflammation of a nerve, sometimes causing paralysis
10. *neur*otic (noo-RAHT-ik): affected by nervous anxiety, phobias, compulsions, and the like
11. peri*meter* (pə-RIM-ə-tər): the outer limits of; the scope or vision of
12. pro*logue* (PROW-*log*): introductory material to either a written work or an oral performance

---

a (*f*at); ay (*f*ate); ah (*f*ar); au (*dou*bt); ch (*ch*ur*ch*); e (*se*lf, *ca*re); ee (*e*vening); ə (*a*bout); f (*f*lag, *ph*one); hw (*wh*ile); i (*f*it); iy (*k*ite); ŋ (li*nk*, si*ng*); o (*au*dio, *cor*n); ow (*o*pen); oo (*coo*k); oi (*oi*l); sh (*sh*oe, ambi*ti*on); th (*th*ink); u (*u*p, l*o*ve); uw (*oo*ze); yu (*cu*re); yuw (*you*th, *u*nited); zh (plea*s*ure)

4. Painful *neuritis* can _____

_____

5. The oversized *metronome* is used for _____

_____

6. An American *agronomist* was sent to _____

_____

7. The architect's preference for *asymmetrical* structures _____

_____

8. Our national level of *gastronomy* _____

_____

9. The weirdest *neologism* I've ever heard is _____

_____

10. An *amorphous* cloud rose out of the swamp and _____

_____

11. The speaker's *prologue* contained _____

_____

12. One normally expects *neurotic* people to be _____

_____

Words from Greek Roots (6)

ROOTS

1. *onym* (word, name):   antonym _____

2. *op(t)* (eye, sight):   optician _____

3. *orth* (right, straight, true):   orthodox _____

4. *pan* (all):   panorama _____

5. *path* (disease, feeling, suffering):   pathetic _____

WORD LIST

1. acr*onym* (AK-rə-*nim*):   a word assembled from the first letters of words in a phrase
2. an*onym*ity (*an*-ə-NIM-ə-tee):   the condition of not being known, especially by name
3. a*path*y (AP-ə-thee):   total absence of caring about anything; indifference
4. em*path*y (EM-pə-thee):   the ability to participate in another's feelings or emotions
5. my*op*ic (miy-AHP-ik):   shortsighted, often in terms of thought
6. *orth*ography (or-THAHG-rə-fee):   the practice of spelling according to standard or accepted rules
7. *orth*opedic (or-thə-PEE-dik):   related to treating problems of the bones, joints, or muscles
8. *pan*acea (*pan*-ə-SEE-ə):   a (supposed) remedy for all problems
9. *pan*chromatic (*pan*-krow-MAT-ik):   sensitive to all visible colors
10. *path*ology (pə-THAHL-ə-jee):   the study of the nature of disease or any variation from a "proper" condition
11. syn*onym*ous (si-NAHN-ə-məs):   having similar or equivalent meaning
12. syn*op*sis (si-NAHP-sis):   a brief summary, as of a novel or play

---

a (*f*a*t*); ay (*f*a*te*); ah (*f*a*r*); au (*d*o*u*bt); ch (*church*); e (*se*lf, *ca*re); ee (*e*v*e*ning); ə (*a*bout); f (*f*lag, *ph*one); hw (*wh*ile); i (*f*i*t*); iy (*k*i*te*); ŋ (li*n*k, si*ng*); o (*au*dio, *cor*n); ow (*o*pen); oo (*c*oo*k*); oi (*oi*l); sh (*sh*oe, ambi*t*ion); th (*th*ink); u (*u*p, l*o*ve); uw (*oo*ze); yu (*cu*re); yuw (*you*th, *u*nited); zh (plea*s*ure)

TRUE-FALSE

_____ 1. One normally expects *myopic* people to be able to see over great distances.

_____ 2. *Panchromatic* patterns are likely to be quite colorful.

_____ 3. A *panacea* may be thought of as a quick solution.

_____ 4. *Synonymous* terms have roughly opposite meanings.

_____ 5. *Anonymity* is the ultimate goal of anyone who seeks public acclaim.

_____ 6. We are likely to feel *empathy* for a loved one who is in distress.

_____ 7. The purpose of a *synopsis* is to summarize.

_____ 8. When we speak of *pathology,* we are usually talking about what is wrong.

_____ 9. *Orthography* deals primarily with how words are pronounced.

_____10. An *acronym* should be a pronounceable series of letters.

_____11. An *orthopedic* specialist is likely to treat a serious heart condition.

_____12. A state of *apathy* usually produces extreme happiness.

SENTENCE FILL-IN

1. I was unable to feel any _____ for the gangster as he lay wounded and bleeding in the street.

2. The doctor found the _____ of my case both interesting and confusing.

3. Such _____ approaches to long-range problems only postpone actions that will ultimately have to be taken.

4. A general _____ toward social change often characterizes those who are well-off.

5. "Scuba" is an _____ for the phrase "self-contained underwater breathing apparatus."

6. Having read only a _____ of the play, I wasn't prepared to discuss the work in any great detail.

7. An _____ surgeon was called in to examine the boy's badly broken leg.

8. The word "profit" should hardly be considered _____ with the word "greed."

9. _____ film should be stored in the refrigerator.

10. There is no easy _____ for the many problems facing our larger cities.

11. It is difficult for a public personality to maintain private _____.

12. English _____ is based primarily on word meaning rather than on word pronunciation.

MATCHING

_____ 1. synopsis

_____ 2. acronym

_____ 3. synonymous

_____ 4. anonymity

_____ 5. pathology

_____ 6. apathy

_____ 7. panchromatic

_____ 8. empathy

_____ 9. panacea

_____ 10. myopic

_____ 11. orthopedic

_____ 12. orthography

a. the ability to participate in another's feelings or emotions

b. sensitive to all visible colors

c. a brief summary, as of a novel or play

d. shortsighted, often in terms of thought

e. a (supposed) remedy for all problems

f. having similar or equivalent meaning

g. a word assembled from the first letters of words in a phrase

h. total absence of caring about anything; indifference

i. the study of the nature of disease or any variation from a "proper" condition

j. the condition of not being known, especially by name

k. related to treating problems of the bones, joints, or muscles

l. the practice of spelling according to standard or accepted rules

SENTENCE COMPLETION

1. A new system of English *orthography* might _____

_____

2. A less expensive *panchromatic* film will _____

_____

3. The *anonymity* of the big city can _____

_____

4. R-rated movies have become *synonymous* with _____

_____

5. A sense of *empathy* suddenly _____

_____

6. NATO is an *acronym* for _____

_____

7. *Orthopedic* doctors can be especially important for _____

_____

8. Political *apathy* sometimes results in _____

_____

9. Roderick's latest *panacea* calls for _____

_____

10. The purpose of medical *pathology* is to _____

_____

11. The *synopsis* was almost as _____

_____

12. Allen's *myopic* squint has resulted in _____

_____

Words from Greek Roots (7)

ROOTS

1. *phil* (love, loving): Philadelphia _____

2. *phos, photo* (light): photograph _____

3. *psych* (mind, spirit): psychology _____

4. *pyr* (fire): Pyrex _____

5. *soph* (wisdom): philosopher _____

WORD LIST

1. *phil*anderer (fi-LAN-dər-ər): a fellow who spends a lot of time engaging in casual love affairs
2. *phil*anthropy (fi-LAN-thrə-pee): the actions of doing good things for other people
3. *phil*atelist (fi-LAT-ə-list): a collector of stamps, especially postage stamps
4. *phos*phorescent (*fahs*-fə-RES-ənt): giving off a glowing light but little heat
5. *photo*mural (*fow*-tə-MYUR-əl): an enlarged photograph attached directly to the surface of a wall
6. *psych*edelic (*siy*-kə-DIL-ik): likely to cause changes in the mind, as hallucinations or delusions
7. *psycho*analysis (*siy*-kow-ə-NAL-ə-sis): the treatment of neuroses through discovery of repressed instinctual forces
8. *psycho*somatic (*siy*-kow-sə-MAT-ik): related to physical problems that arise from the mind or the emotions
9. *pyre* (PIYR): a heap of wood on which a dead body is cremated
10. *pyro*maniac (*piy*-rə-MAY-nee-*ak*): one who gets (sexual) pleasure from starting fires
11. *soph*isticated (sə-FIS-tə-*kay*-tid): wise; aware of the ways of the world
12. *sopho*moric (*sahf*-ə-MOR-ik): of the arrogant immaturity arising from a little learning

---

a (f*a*t); ay (f*a*te); ah (f*a*r); au (d*ou*bt); ch (*ch*ur*ch*); e (s*e*lf, c*a*re); ee (*e*vening); ə (*a*bout); f (*f*lag, *ph*one); hw (*wh*ile); i (f*i*t); iy (k*i*te); ŋ (li*nk*, si*ng*); o (*au*dio, c*o*rn); ow (*o*pen); oo (c*oo*k); oi (*oi*l); sh (*sh*oe, ambi*ti*on); th (*th*ink); u (*u*p, l*o*ve); uw (*oo*ze); yu (c*u*re); yuw (*you*th, *u*nited); zh (plea*s*ure)

117

TRUE-FALSE

_____ 1. Various methods of *psychoanalysis* are employed by psychiatrists.

_____ 2. *Photomurals* can usually move and speak.

_____ 3. *Philanthropy* should grow out of a love for one's fellow creatures.

_____ 4. One normally expects a *philanderer* to take love affairs very seriously.

_____ 5. *Psychosomatic* illnesses are never serious.

_____ 6. One of the characteristics of *psychedelic* drugs is that they can produce hallucinations.

_____ 7. A *phosphorescent* glow is likely to produce great heat.

_____ 8. Most states use the funeral *pyre* to dispose of unclaimed cadavers.

_____ 9. We normally expect the young to have something of a *sophomoric* view of life.

_____10. A book of matches can pose a great temptation for a *pyromaniac*.

_____11. A *philatelist* makes a hobby of stuffing wild animals.

_____12. *Sophisticated* people are those among us who know what makes the world go 'round.

SENTENCE FILL-IN

1. _____ seem to have become a popular medium of decoration in many contemporary museums.

2. The reporter was no naive little girl; she was a _____ newspaper correspondent.

3. _____ ailments are nonetheless real to those who suffer from them.

4. God help the _____ who tries to keep up with all the new commemorative stamps.

5. A _____ does not normally indulge in arson for profit.

6. A lifelong _____, Neville seems incapable of a permanent relationship with a woman.

7. Your _____ contentions will be destroyed under the scrutiny of real pros in the field.

8. _____ drugs were an "in" item during the late 1960s and early 1970s.

9. Our tax system makes public _____ very profitable for the wealthy.

10. _____ assumes, perhaps falsely, that knowing the source of mental illness will assist in its cure.

11. After a solemn ceremony, the tribal chief's body was placed on a large funeral

_____.

12. The neon tetra's _____ stripe makes it a popular little fish for home aquariums.

MATCHING

_____ 1. *sopho*moric

_____ 2. *phil*anderer

_____ 3. *soph*isticated

_____ 4. *phil*anthropy

_____ 5. *pyro*maniac

_____ 6. *phil*atelist

_____ 7. *pyre*

_____ 8. *phos*phorescent

_____ 9. *psycho*somatic

_____ 10. *photo*mural

_____ 11. *psycho*analysis

_____ 12. *psych*edelic

a. giving off a glowing light but little heat
b. a heap of wood on which a dead body is cremated
c. the actions of doing good things for other people
d. wise; aware of the ways of the world
e. a fellow who spends a lot of time engaging in casual love affairs
f. likely to cause changes in the mind, as hallucinations or delusions
g. of the arrogant immaturity arising from a little learning
h. a collector of stamps, especially postage stamps
i. one who gets (sexual) pleasure from starting fires
j. related to physical problems that arise from the mind or the emotions
k. an enlarged photograph attached directly to the surface of a wall
l. the treatment of neuroses through discovery of repressed instinctual forces

SENTENCE COMPLETION

1. A string of *pyres* _____

_____

2. The hall's *psychedelic* lights gradually _____

_____

3. One is always disappointed by so *sophomoric* a performance by _____

_____

4. The popular image of a *philanderer* has it that _____

_____

5. True *philanthropy* never _____

_____

6. *Psychoanalysis* seems to be very popular among _____

_____

7. Having been a *philatelist* for many years, Jennifer _____

_____

8. *Psychosomatic* illnesses among _____

_____

9. As more *sophisticated* weapons systems are built, _____

_____

10. A *phosphorescent* aura surrounded _____

_____

11. There may be just a little of the *pyromaniac* in _____

_____

12. One of the most grotesque *photomurals* I have ever seen was _____

_____

Words from Greek Roots (8)

ROOTS

1. *techn* (art, skill): technique _____

2. *tele* (far): television _____

3. *the* (God): monotheism _____

4. *therm* (heat): thermostat _____

5. *tox* (poison): toxic _____

WORD LIST

1. a*the*istic (*ay*-thee-IS-tik): not believing in the existence of God
2. de*tox*ify (dee-TAHK-sə-*fiy*): to remove the poisons from; to purify
3. dia*therm*y (DIY-ə-*thur*-mee): medical treatment in which heat is directed into body tissues
4. pan*the*ism (PAN-thee-*iz*-əm): the notion (doctrine) that God is manifest in all things
5. pyro*techn*ics (*piy*-rə-TEK-niks): the art of making or displaying fireworks; any brilliant display
6. *techn*ology (tek-NAHL-ə-jee): the application of pure science to the handling of specific engineering problems
7. *tele*genic (*tel*-ə-JEN-ik): having physical characteristics that project well on television
8. *tele*metry (tə-LEM-ə-tree): the automatic processes of determining the location of distant objects through transmitted data
9. *tele*pathy (tə-LEP-ə-thee): (mystical) nonverbal communication between minds
10. *the*ology (thee-AHL-ə-jee): the systematic study of God and all matters religious or divine
11. *therm*al (THUR-məl): related in any way to heat or warmth
12. *tox*icology (*tahk*-sə-KAHL-ə-jee): the science of poisons: their detection, effects, antidotes, and so on

---

a (fat); ay (fate); ah (far); au (doubt); ch (church); e (self, care); ee (evening); ə (about); f (flag, phone); hw (while); i (fit); iy (kite); ŋ (link, sing); o (audio, corn); ow (open); oo (cook); oi (oil); sh (shoe, ambition); th (think); u (up, love); uw (ooze); yu (cure); yuw (youth, united); zh (pleasure)

121

TRUE-FALSE

_____ 1. *Toxicology* concerns itself primarily with the study of public transportation systems.

_____ 2. One normally expects a preacher to have studied *theology*.

_____ 3. *Diathermy* involves the treatment of muscles with running water.

_____ 4. When we *detoxify* something, we severely pollute it.

_____ 5. The flash and boom of *pyrotechnics* often seem to imitate a battle in the air.

_____ 6. The products of *technology* tend to be mechanical rather than philosophical.

_____ 7. *Atheistic* people have always hated God.

_____ 8. *Telepathy* involves only verbal (spoken) communication.

_____ 9. *Thermal* underwear is likely to sell better in Michigan than in Alabama.

_____10. *Pantheism* and atheism are virtually the same thing.

_____11. Modern *telemetry* systems make extensive use of computers.

_____12. A *telegenic* appearance is likely to be characterized by features that disgust people.

SENTENCE FILL-IN

1. _____ does not appear to be a method of communication used by great numbers of people.

2. These new _____ windows have three separate panes of glass.

3. With the continued dissemination of new and more complex chemicals, _____ becomes an ever more important science.

4. College students sometimes complain that courses in _____ destroy their religious faith.

5. Fourth of July celebrations often conclude with spectacular performances of

_____ .

6. An accurate system of _____ is a necessity for any space flight.

7. The team trainer prescribed _____ treatments for the athlete's injured shoulder.

122

8. Classical _____ saw manifestations of God in all things.

9. Only the most _____ models are used by television advertisers.

10. One of the ironies of modern _____ is that it can do almost everything but turn itself off.

11. Any society that rejects a belief in God and places its faith in the possession of pleasurable objects is essentially _____.

12. While these factories continue to spew out poisons, it will be impossible to _____ the local environment.

MATCHING

_____ 1. *tox*icology

_____ 2. a*the*istic

_____ 3. *therm*al

_____ 4. de*tox*ify

_____ 5. *the*ology

_____ 6. dia*therm*y

_____ 7. *tele*pathy

_____ 8. pan*the*ism

_____ 9. *tele*metry

_____ 10. pyro*techn*ics

_____ 11. *tele*genic

_____ 12. *techn*ology

a. (mystical) nonverbal communication between minds

b. related in any way to heat or warmth

c. to remove the poisons from; to purify

d. the application of pure science to the handling of specific engineering problems

e. the art of making or displaying fireworks; any brilliant display

f. the notion (doctrine) that God is manifest in all things

g. not believing in the existence of God

h. the science of poisons: their detection, effects, antidotes, and so on

i. the systematic study of God and all matters religious or divine

j. having physical characteristics that project well on television

k. medical treatment in which heat is directed into body tissues

l. the automatic processes of determining the location of distant objects through transmitted data

SENTENCE COMPLETION

1. What a display of *pyrotechnics* the golfers put on when they _____

_____

2. The most *telegenic* candidate will _____

_____

3. *Atheistic* arguments are not likely to be very popular among _____

_____

4. *Thermal* blankets are a must for _____

_____

5. More advanced systems of *telemetry* will be needed when _____

_____

6. One more session of *diathermy* and I'll _____

_____

7. *Pantheistic* doctrine is consistent with many _____

_____

8. Dr. Austin, an eminent *toxicologist,* maintains that _____

_____

9. *Telepathic* signals may be able to _____

_____

10. Several hours of quiet rest were needed to *detoxify* the _____

_____

11. If you make *theology* too scientific, the result _____

_____

12. As our *technology* becomes more advanced, we will _____

_____

Chapter 3

Words with Prefixes

Prefixes are clusters of letters that come at the beginnings of words. Quite often, when they are of Latin or Greek derivation, prefixes are actually old prepositions that now join with roots—and subsequently with suffixes—to form words.

This chapter contains twelve sequences of exercises, each concentrating on a list of derivatives developed from the group of prefixes at the beginning of the sequence. Unlike the chapters dealing with Latin and Greek roots, this chapter contains sequences with varying numbers of prefixes *and* varying numbers of derivatives of each prefix. As in the Latin and Greek chapters, however, the derivatives have the prefixes italicized for easy identification.

A further distinction of this chapter is that the prefixes are placed into three categories. These categories distinguish among prefixes which indicate (1) time and position, (2) quality and condition, and (3) number and amount. There are seven sequences of exercises with prefixes indicating time and position; four sequences with prefixes indicating quality and condition; and one sequence with prefixes indicating number and amount. Otherwise, the actual working of the exercises in the sequences requires exactly the same performance as the exercises in the Latin and Greek chapters.

You will notice that a few prefixes change their spelling when they are attached to words or roots beginning with certain sounds. This process is called assimilation, and such prefixes are called *assimilating prefixes*. The assimilating prefixes taken up in this chapter include *ad-*, *com-*, *ex-*, *in-*, *ob-*, and *syn-*. Two examples of assimilating prefixes, *ad-* and *com-*, are shown in the following chart:

_____ 3. To *admonish* is to accept criticism casually.

_____ 4. An *attenuated* appearance is likely to be the result of poor health.

_____ 5. To *aggrandize* one's sphere of influence is to increase it.

_____ 6. One normally expects an *assignation* to take place in private.

_____ 7. To be in *arrears* is to be well read.

_____ 8. We *acclimate* ourselves to a region when we refuse to live there.

_____ 9. A natural *affinity* for anything most often produces a dislike.

_____10. To *annihilate* enemies is to destroy them completely.

_____11. To *acquiesce* is to put up a fight.

_____12. To *annul* is to void.

SENTENCE FILL-IN

1. Although the senator admitted having had an _____ with the young woman, he maintained that nothing improper had occurred.

2. Although Ruth isn't actually a genius, she does have a natural _____ for mathematics.

3. History seems to teach that military _____ brings only temporary peace.

4. Sooner or later freshmen must _____ themselves to life on a college campus.

5. America's _____ international posture is not improved by continued devaluation of the dollar.

6. If you are serious about improving your grades, you must _____ more time for study.

7. As an old friend, I _____ you to take better care of your family.

8. A single one of these bombs could _____ New York City.

9. The president will hardly _____ his position by appointing mediocre subordinates.

10. As usual, I'm in _____ with my car payment.

11. It might be wise to _____ to so sage a criticism.

12. How ironic it is that a single blunder can _____ so many previous wise decisions.

MATCHING

_____ 1. *at*tenuated

_____ 2. *ac*climate

_____ 3. *as*signation

_____ 4. *ac*quiesce

_____ 5. *ar*rears

_____ 6. *ad*monish

_____ 7. *ap*peasement

_____ 8. *af*finity

_____ 9. *an*nul

_____10. *ag*grandize

_____11. *an*nihilate

_____12. *al*locate

a. a seemingly inborn attraction or interest
b. to make no longer valid; to put an end to
c. the condition of having not met a responsibility on time
d. to adjust to a different (new) set of circumstances
e. to reduce to nothing; to destroy totally
f. having become slender, diluted, weak, or feeble
g. a secret meeting, as between lovers
h. to give in without protest; to agree quietly
i. to caution mildly; to urge
j. to put aside for a specific purpose
k. relenting in response to (hostile) demands in order to keep the peace
l. to make (appear) greater, as in power, stature, or sphere of influence

SENTENCE COMPLETION

1. My father-in-law threatened to *annul* the marriage if _____

_____

2. Your apparent *affinity* for catastrophe makes _____

_____

3. Shawn refuses to *acquiesce* to such _____

_____

4. This sordid *assignation* of yours will _____

_____

5. Every four years it seems that we must again *acclimate* ourselves to _____

_____

6. The child's *attenuated* attention span was _____

_____

7. Far in *arrears* with his obligations, Bradley _____

   _____

8. The speaker *admonished* her audience to _____

   _____

9. We must *allocate* sufficient _____

   _____

10. Our *appeasement* of the terrorists resulted in _____

    _____

11. Perhaps we can *aggrandize* our image by _____

    _____

12. By *annihilating* our more vocal opponents, we _____

    _____

Words with Prefixes (2)
Time and Position

PREFIXES

1. *ab(s)-* (from, from off): abduct, abstract _____

2. *ante-* (before, in front of): antedate _____

3. *apo-* (away from, off): apologize _____

4. *cata-* (down, downward): catalogue _____

5. *circum-* (around): circumnavigation _____

WORD LIST

1. *ab*dicate (AB-də-*kayt*): to renounce or deny, usually openly or formally
2. *ab*original (ab-ə-RIJ-ə-nəl): native to an area from earliest times
3. *abs*truse (ab-STRUWS): deep and complex; thus, difficult to understand
4. *ante*cedent (an-ti-SEED-ənt): occurring at a time prior to another incident
5. *ante*diluvian (an-ti-də-LUW-vee-ən): literally, from before the Biblical Flood; thus, out of date and old-fashioned
6. *apo*calyptic (ə-*pahk*-ə-LIP-tik): related to dramatic revelations and prophecies
7. *apo*cryphal (ə-PAK-rə-fəl): of questionable authenticity; counterfeit
8. *cata*combs (KAT-ə-*kowmz*): a series of underground chambers or tunnels, usually with places for graves
9. *cata*lyst (KAT-əl-ist): a substance or person that makes possible the uniting of other substances or persons
10. *circum*scribe (SUR-kəm-*skriyb*): to mark off (very specifically) what is intended or required; to confine or limit
11. *circum*spect (SUR-kəm-*spekt*): very careful in considering all matters before acting
12. *circum*vent (*sur*-kəm-VENT): to get the better of, as by crafty diversion; to go around

---

a (*f*at); ay (*f*ate); ah (*f*ar); au (*d*oubt); ch (*church*); e (*se*lf, *c*are); ee (*e*vening); ə (*a*bout); f (*f*lag, *ph*one); hw (*wh*ile); i (*fi*t); iy (*k*ite); ŋ (li*nk*, si*ng*); o (*au*dio, *c*orn); ow (*o*pen); oo (*c*ook); oi (*oi*l); sh (*sh*oe, ambi*ti*on); th (*th*ink); u (*u*p, l*o*ve); uw (*oo*ze); yu (*c*ure); yuw (*you*th, *u*nited); zh (plea*s*ure)

TRUE-FALSE

_____ 1. *Apocryphal* tears must be shed in earnest.

_____ 2. An *abstruse* explanation is easily understood.

_____ 3. People often try to *circumvent* laws they do not wish to abide by.

_____ 4. The *circumspect* individual seldom does anything on impulse.

_____ 5. An *aboriginal* plant is one that has been imported.

_____ 6. *Apocalyptic* utterances most often deal with the distant past.

_____ 7. *Catacombs* are always underground.

_____ 8. If your proposal is *antecedent* to mine, you must have made yours before I made mine.

_____ 9. An *antediluvian* point of view must be very modern.

_____10. One can use a *catalyst* to make things move along more smoothly.

_____11. To *circumscribe* is to confuse what is false and what is true.

_____12. To *abdicate* is to insist upon getting one's own way.

SENTENCE FILL-IN

1. The notion of individual human worth must be _____ to the establishment of a democratic government.

2. It has become practically impossible to _____ all the red tape involved in trying to land a government contract.

3. Most people in the audience dismissed the mystic's remarks as wild _____ surmises.

4. Good will is the _____ that can make many a difficult enterprise prosper.

5. The government's new tax laws are so _____ that even the IRS representative doesn't understand them.

6. Walking through the _____, we came upon a whole tribe of dry bones.

7. The search committee should be very _____ in choosing a new department head.

8. Hopefully, notions of racial and sexual inferiority will soon go the way of other such _____ ideas of the past.

9. New Zealand's _____ tribes date from the Stone Age.

10. Many of these tales of the movie star's childhood are _____ and shouldn't be believed.

11. It is no easy task to _____ with absolute precision what the nation's foreign policy should be.

12. Far too many parents seem willing to _____ the responsibility for disciplining their children.

MATCHING

_____ 1. *circum*vent

_____ 2. *ab*dicate

_____ 3. *circum*spect

_____ 4. *ab*original

_____ 5. *circum*scribe

_____ 6. *ab*struse

_____ 7. *cata*lyst

_____ 8. *ante*cedent

_____ 9. *cata*combs

_____10. *ante*diluvian

_____11. *apo*cryphal

_____12. *apo*calyptic

a. of questionable authenticity; counterfeit
b. native to an area from earliest times
c. occurring at a time prior to another incident
d. a substance or person that makes possible the uniting of other substances or persons
e. very careful in considering all matters before acting
f. to renounce or deny, usually openly or formally
g. deep and complex; thus, difficult to understand
h. to get the better of, as by crafty diversion; to go around
i. related to dramatic revelations and prophecies
j. to mark off (very specifically) what is intended or required; to confine or limit
k. literally, from before the Biblical Flood; thus, out of date and old-fashioned
l. a series of underground chambers or tunnels, usually with places for graves

SENTENCE COMPLETION

1. These claims are too *apocryphal* to _____

_____

2. Our *antecedent* prejudices sometimes _____

_____

3. You will not *circumvent* the truth by _____

_____

4. The weekend *extravaganza* included _____

_____

5. The *irritant* was finally removed by _____

_____

6. Few *extroverts* are _____

_____

7. Hardly an *internecine* conflict, the _____

_____

8. The prospects of *imminent* wealth might _____

_____

9. Please take the little time needed to *intercede* for _____

_____

10. If *extraterrestrial* beings ever do _____

_____

11. A confirmed *introvert,* Sigmund almost never _____

_____

12. Several *intramural* clubs have _____

_____

Words with Prefixes (6)
Time and Position

PREFIXES

*1. *ob-, oc-, op-* (toward, facing, against): obstacle, occasion, opposition _____

_____

2. *para-* (alongside): paramedic _____

3. *peri-* (around): periscope _____

4. *post-* (after, later): postscript _____

WORD LIST

1. *ob*lique (ə-BLEEK): not straightforward or to the point; indirect and evasive
2. *ob*livion (ə-BLIV-ee-ən): a condition in which the mind forgets everything
3. *oc*cluded (ə-KLUWD-id): closed shut, stopped up, or blocked
4. *oc*cult (ə-KULT): beyond the range of ordinary knowledge; mysterious, concealed, or secret
5. *op*portune (*ahp*-ər-TUWN): the most suitable, appropriate, or accommodating
6. *op*pression (ə-PRESH-ən): an unjust exercise of authority over another; a feeling of intense distress
7. *para*plegic (*par*-ə-PLEE-jik): a person paralyzed in the lower half of the body
8. *para*professional (*par*-ə-prə-FESH-ə-nəl): a worker who assists a professional person
9. *peri*patetic (*per*-i-pə-TET-ik): walking or moving from place to place; unsettled
10. *peri*pheral (pə-RIF-ər-əl): away from the center (of activity); of minor importance
11. *post*humous (PAHS-chə-məs): (taking place) after death
12. *post*partum (*powst*-PAHR-təm): related to the period just after childbirth

---

a (*fat*); ay (*fate*); ah (*far*); au (*doubt*); ch (*church*); e (*self, care*); ee (*evening*); ə (*about*); f (*flag, phone*); hw (*while*); i (*fit*); iy (*kite*); ŋ (*link, sing*); o (*audio, corn*); ow (*open*); oo (*cook*); oi (*oil*); sh (*shoe, ambition*); th (*think*); u (*up, love*); uw (*ooze*); yu (*cure*); yuw (*youth, united*); zh (*pleasure*)

TRUE-FALSE

_____ 1. Today many colleges offer *paraprofessional* degrees.

_____ 2. Items of *peripheral* importance are likely to be incidental.

_____ 3. *Oblivion* is a state of mental alertness.

_____ 4. The *opportune* moment to do something is usually the wrong time.

_____ 5. *Postpartum* discomfort occurs only during pregnancy.

_____ 6. In the Middle Ages, chemistry was generally viewed as an *occult* activity.

_____ 7. An *oblique* statement is likely to be straightforward and to the point.

_____ 8. *Peripatetic* individuals are usually calm and sedate.

_____ 9. One normally expects a *paraplegic* to get around in a wheelchair.

_____10. Too much *posthumous* praise can ruin a young writer's chances of maturing.

_____11. Feelings of *oppression* can make one very unhappy.

_____12. An *occluded* vein has some sort of blockage.

SENTENCE FILL-IN

1. A society as _____ as ours keeps hundreds of moving and storage companies in business.

2. _____ glory was of little comfort to the artist who shot himself.

3. The witness's _____ responses raised more questions than they answered.

4. The conglomerate patiently waited for the most _____ time to buy up the stock of the small manufacturing company.

5. _____ aides are used by many school systems to assist teachers.

6. As they were described in the press, the _____ teachings of the strange religious sect bewildered the average reader.

7. _____ infection was once a dreaded killer of women.

8. The _____ of intoxication is seldom complete.

9. A _____ creature, the hawk lives distant from the buzz of urban civilization.

148

10. Though a _____ since a skiing accident, Harriet nonetheless leads an active life.

11. According to the television news, political _____ is still a fact of life in many Third World nations.

12. The weather forecaster said that the _____ front would produce some severe thunderstorms.

MATCHING

_____ 1. *post*partum

_____ 2. *ob*lique

_____ 3. *post*humous

_____ 4. *ob*livion

_____ 5. *peri*pheral

_____ 6. *oc*cluded

_____ 7. *peri*patetic

_____ 8. *oc*cult

_____ 9. *para*professional

_____ 10. *op*portune

_____ 11. *para*plegic

_____ 12. *op*pression

a. (taking place) after death
b. walking or moving from place to place; unsettled
c. a person paralyzed in the lower half of the body
d. the most suitable, appropriate, or accommodating
e. closed shut, stopped up, or blocked
f. a condition in which the mind forgets everything
g. not straightforward or to the point; indirect and evasive
h. related to the period just after childbirth
i. a worker who assists a professional person
j. beyond the range of ordinary knowledge; mysterious, concealed, or secret
k. away from the center (of activity); of minor importance
l. an unjust exercise of authority over another; a feeling of intense distress

SENTENCE COMPLETION

1. The medium's pretensions to *occult* powers were _____

_____

2. *Postpartum* depression is a _____

_____

3. How *opportune* it would be for _____

_____

149

4. Our legal system is beginning to use many *paraprofessionals* to _____

_____

5. Such *oblique* lessons are hardly _____

_____

6. As a *peripheral* concern, _____

_____

7. The *posthumous* publication of _____

_____

8. Strangely enough, *oblivion* followed the novelist's _____

_____

9. *Paraplegics* often have their handicap made even more difficult to manage by _____

_____

10. The *peripatetic* movements of the insects reminded me of _____

_____

11. The doctor said the *occlusion* was caused by _____

_____

12. Continued economic *oppression* of minorities may _____

_____

Words with Prefixes (7)
Time and Position

PREFIXES

1. *pre-* (before, in front of):   precede _____

2. *pro-* (forward, ahead of):   progress _____

3. *re-, retro-* (back, again, backward):   retract, retroactive _____

_____

4. *se-* (away, apart from):   secret _____

5. *trans-* (across, through, over):   transport _____

_____

WORD LIST

1. *pre*cocious (pri-KOW-shəs):   developed or matured ahead of time
2. *pre*monition (*pree*-mə-NISH-ən):   an advance vision or forewarning, usually that something bad will happen
3. *pro*fuse (prə-FYUWS):   pouring forth in generous or excessive quantities
4. *pro*menade (*prahm*-ə-NAYD):   to walk about, as for pleasure or casual exercise; a leisurely walk
5. *re*ciprocal (ri-SIP-rə-kəl):   affecting both sides mutually, usually to the advantage of both
6. *re*surgence (ri-SUR-jəns):   coming once again to life or force
7. *retro*grade (RE-trə-*grayd*):   turning (moving) backward
8. *retro*spect (RE-trə-*spekt*):   a view back on things that have already occurred
9. *se*cede (si-SEED):   to withdraw from; to leave
10. *se*duce (si-DUWS):   to lead astray or persuade to do something less than upright
11. *trans*pose (trans-POWS):   to reverse the normal order of, as words or figures
12. *trans*verse (trans-VURS):   from side to side; crosswise

_____

a (*f*a*t*); ay (*f*a*te*); ah (*f*a*r*); au (*d*ou*bt*); ch (*church*); e (*se*l*f*, *c*a*re*); ee (*evening*); ə (*about*); f (*f*lag, *ph*one); hw (*wh*ile); i (*f*i*t*); iy (*k*i*te*); ŋ (li*nk*, si*ng*); o (*au*dio, *c*o*rn*); ow (*open*); oo (*c*oo*k*); oi (*oi*l); sh (*sh*oe, ambi*ti*on); th (*th*ink); u (*u*p, l*o*ve); uw (*ooze*); yu (*cu*re); yuw (*youth*, *u*nited); zh (plea*s*ure)

TRUE-FALSE

_____ 1. To *promenade* is to daydream.

_____ 2. *Retrograde* movements are always circular.

_____ 3. To *seduce* is to attempt to corrupt.

_____ 4. A *premonition* is a vague dream of the past.

_____ 5. Anything situated in a *transverse* position is upside down.

_____ 6. *Precocious* abilities are usually slow to reveal themselves.

_____ 7. To *secede* is to do better than anyone else.

_____ 8. To *transpose* words is to read them in reverse order.

_____ 9. *Profuse* praise is likely to be excessive.

_____10. A *resurgence* is the final gasp of a declining enterprise.

_____11. We often see things more clearly in *retrospect.*

_____12. *Reciprocal* agreements involve two or more parties.

SENTENCE FILL-IN

1. If an instructor is too _____ with disapproving criticism, students are likely to become hesitant in their work.

2. A sudden _____ movement of the machine's power unit quickly pinned the unsuspecting technician.

3. A _____ child, Susan learned to read at the age of four.

4. A _____ mounting of the engine saved more than a foot in the car's overall length.

5. The Constitution does not allow a state to _____ from the Union.

6. Several people in the community maintained that they had had a _____ of disaster a week before the dam burst.

7. If you _____ these two adjectives, the expression becomes ambiguous.

8. Japan's economic _____ since World War II has been mind boggling.

9. Don't try to _____ me with praise; I prefer money.

10. An evening _____ in the park has become a ritual for the retired letter carrier.

11. Political bedfellows often engage in _____ backscratching.

12. In _____, the summer stock production of *Hamlet* seems rather amateurish.

MATCHING

_____ 1. *trans*verse

_____ 2. *pre*cocious

_____ 3. *trans*pose

_____ 4. *pre*monition

_____ 5. *se*duce

_____ 6. *pro*fuse

_____ 7. *se*cede

_____ 8. *pro*menade

_____ 9. *retro*spect

_____ 10. *re*ciprocal

_____ 11. *retro*grade

_____ 12. *re*surgence

a. to walk about, as for pleasure or casual exercise; a leisurely walk

b. pouring forth in generous or excessive quantities

c. developed or matured ahead of time

d. coming once again to life or force

e. turning (moving) backward

f. to reverse the normal order of, as words or figures

g. to lead astray or persuade to do something less than upright

h. a view back on things that have already occurred

i. from side to side; crosswise

j. to withdraw from; to leave

k. affecting both sides mutually, usually to the advantage of both

l. an advance vision or forewarning, usually that something bad will happen

SENTENCE COMPLETION

1. *Reciprocal* trade among the Common Market countries has _____

_____

2. It is the job of Madison Avenue to *seduce* the _____

_____

3. In *retrospect,* my initial position _____

_____

4. The machine's *transverse* armature was used to _____

_____

153

5. My first *premonition* occurred just after _____

_____

6. A *resurgent* interest in the supernatural has led _____

_____

7. If Quebec is able to *secede* from the rest of Canada, _____

_____

8. *Profuse* in her praise of the project, Mercedes said _____

_____

9. The *retrograde* spinning of _____

_____

10. A mistaken *transposition* of sentences resulted in _____

_____

11. Few creatures of the animal world are more *precocious* than _____

_____

12. The *promenade* concerts in the park have become _____

_____

Words with Prefixes (8)
Quality and Condition

PREFIXES

1. *a-, an-* (not, without):   asexual, anesthetic _____

2. *ant(i)-* (in opposition to):   antacid, anticlimax _____

3. *contra-, contro-, counter-* (opposed to):   contradiction, controversy, counterpart _____

_____

4. *dis-* (not):   disloyal _____

5. *eu-* (good, well):   eulogy _____

WORD LIST

1. *a*moral (ay-MOR-əl):   without the ordinary ability to distinguish right from wrong
2. *an*emic (ə-NEEM-ik):   without healthy coloration or vitality
3. *ant*agonistic (an-*tag*-ə-NIS-tik):   actively (angrily) in opposition to
4. *anti*social (*an*-ti-SOW-shəl):   generally unfriendly toward other people; hostile
5. *contra*band (KAHN-trə-*band*):   goods bought and sold illegally
6. *contro*vert (KAHN-trə-*vurt*):   to argue in opposition to; to oppose in debate
7. *counter*mand (*kaun*-tər-MAND):   to cancel or revoke, as a previous order; a command reversing an earlier order
8. *counter*productive (*kaun*-tər-prə-DUK-tiv):   characteristic of activities whose results are contrary to those presumably intended
9. *dis*array (*dis*-ə-RAY):   a condition of confusion, untidiness, or disorder
10. *dis*enchanted (*dis*-in-CHANT-id):   no longer under the power of; disappointed with
11. *eu*phoria (yuw-FOR-ee-ə):   a feeling of extreme well-being; an emotional "high"
12. *eu*thanasia (*yuw*-thə-NAY-zhə):   a painless (easy) death or killing

---

a (f*a*t);   ay (f*a*te);   ah (f*a*r);   au (d*ou*bt);   ch (*ch*ur*ch*);   e (s*e*lf, c*a*re);   ee (*e*vening);   ə (*a*bout);   f (*f*lag, *ph*one);   hw (*wh*ile);   i (f*i*t);   iy (k*i*te);   ŋ (li*n*k, si*ng*);   o (*au*dio, c*o*rn);   ow (*o*pen);   oo (c*oo*k);   oi (*oi*l);   sh (*sh*oe, ambi*ti*on);   th (*th*ink);   u (*u*p, l*o*ve);   uw (*oo*ze);   yu (c*u*re);   yuw (*you*th, *u*nited);   zh (plea*s*ure)

TRUE-FALSE

_____ 1. Color television sets are an example of a *contraband* item of trade.

_____ 2. To *countermand* an instruction or procedure is to reverse it.

_____ 3. An *anemic* child is usually robust and full of fun.

_____ 4. *Antisocial* behavior is likely to be hostile.

_____ 5. *Amoral* people are driven to do only what is right and proper.

_____ 6. To *controvert* a statement is to agree with it.

_____ 7. Liquor sometimes produces a state of *euphoria*.

_____ 8. *Antagonistic* behavior is likely to incur opposition.

_____ 9 To be *disenchanted* is to be pleasantly mystified.

_____10. Death by firing squad is hardly an example of *euthanasia*.

_____11. A condition of *disarray* suggests careful planning and organization.

_____12. A *counterproductive* activity will most likely come to nothing.

SENTENCE FILL-IN

1. Why must someone _____ every opinion I express?

2. _____ offers us a pleasant way to go—when we go.

3. Is corporate behavior that ignores human compassion _____ or immoral?

4. The _____ of unexpected wealth is sometimes short-lived.

5. Such _____ tactics will hardly persuade people to cooperate with you.

6. The general has the authority to _____ any orders given by his subordinate officers.

7. Our attempts to provide a decent life-style for senior citizens are so _____ as to be a national disgrace.

8. Cocaine and marijuana are still _____ commodities in every state.

9. The young man's antagonistic remarks were further evidence of his _____ behavior.

10. Many of our citizens have become _____ with the government's empty promises of tax reform.

11. In almost any occupation, constant bickering and argumentation are

_____.

12. Following the power blackout during the rush hour, the city was in an incredible state

of _____.

MATCHING

_____ 1. *eu*thanasia

_____ 2. *a*moral

_____ 3. *eu*phoria

_____ 4. *an*emic

_____ 5. *dis*enchanted

_____ 6. *ant*agonistic

_____ 7. *dis*array

_____ 8. *anti*social

_____ 9. *counter*productive

_____ 10. *contra*band

_____ 11. *counter*mand

_____ 12. *contro*vert

a. actively (angrily) in opposition to
b. without healthy coloration or vitality
c. to argue in opposition to; to oppose in debate
d. a painless (easy) death or killing
e. goods bought and sold illegally
f. a condition of confusion, untidiness, or disorder
g. to cancel or revoke, as a previous order; a command reversing an earlier order
h. without the ordinary ability to distinguish right from wrong
i. a feeling of extreme well-being; an emotional "high"
j. no longer under the power of; disappointed with
k. generally unfriendly toward other people; hostile
l. characteristic of activities whose results are contrary to those presumably intended

SENTENCE COMPLETION

1. The company's books were in *disarray* from _____

_____

2. Though dealing in *contraband* can be profitable, _____

_____

3. *Anemic* from improper diet, the children _____

_____

4. Though seemingly *counterproductive* at the time, the _____

   _____

5. It is nothing short of *amoral* to _____

   _____

6. The teacher said the child had *antisocial* tendencies just because _____

   _____

7. If we could only *controvert* the _____

   _____

8. The *euphoria* of the first victory was quickly _____

   _____

9. The two old *antagonists* were _____

   _____

10. The type of *euthanasia* practiced at _____

    _____

11. The unexpected *countermand* came as _____

    _____

12. *Disenchanted* with school because _____

    _____

Words with Prefixes (9)
Quality and Condition

PREFIXES

1. *heter(o)-* (other, different):   heterodox _____

2. *hom(o)-* (same, alike):   homosexual _____

3. *hyper-* (excessive):   hypersensitive _____

4. *hypo-* (less than, under):   hypodermic _____

5. *mal-* (bad, evil):   malpractice _____

WORD LIST

1. *hetero*geneous (*het-ər-ə-JEE-nee-əs*):   composed of elements or items which are unlike
2. *heter*onym (HET-ər-ə-*nim*):   a word with the same spelling as another, but with a different pronunciation and meaning
3. *homo*genize (hə-MAHJ-ə-*niyz*):   to make uniform throughout
4. *hom*onym (HAHM-ə-*nim*):   a word with the same pronunciation as another, but with different spelling and meaning
5. *hyper*active (*hiy*-pər-AK-tiv):   abnormally high-strung; unable to remain stationary
6. *hyper*bole (hiy-PUR-bə-lee):   an exaggeration of the literal facts
7. *hyper*tension (*hiy*-pər-TEN-shən):   high blood pressure
8. *hypo*critical (*hip*-ə-KRIT-i-kəl):   pretending to be more virtuous than one is
9. *hypo*thesis (hiy-PAHTH-ə-sis):   a yet-to-be-proved assumption
10. *mal*evolent (mə-LEV-ə-lənt):   wishing bad things to happen to other people; showing ill will
11. *mal*feasance (mal-FEE-zəns):   misconduct, especially by a person in public office
12. *mal*ignancy (mə-LIG-nən-see):   an evil or harmful growth or condition

---

a (f*at*);   ay (f*ate*);   ah (f*ar*);   au (d*ou*bt);   ch (*church*);   e (s*e*lf, c*a*re);   ee (*e*vening);   ə (*a*bout);   f (*f*lag, *ph*one);   hw (*wh*ile);   i (f*i*t);   iy (k*i*te);   ŋ (li*n*k, si*ng*);   o (*au*dio, c*or*n);   ow (*o*pen);   oo (c*oo*k);   oi (*oi*l);   sh (*sh*oe, ambi*ti*on);   th (*th*ink);   u (*u*p, l*o*ve);   uw (*oo*ze);   yu (c*u*re);   yuw (*y*outh, *u*nited);   zh (plea*s*ure)

TRUE-FALSE

_____ 1. To *homogenize* something is to remove all the impurities from it.

_____ 2. Discovered *malfeasance* is likely to destroy a civil servant's public image.

_____ 3. The word "laugh" is a *homonym* of the word "calf."

_____ 4. One can expect *hypocritical* people to be extremely intolerant of others' faults.

_____ 5. The population of a city like New York is *heterogeneous*.

_____ 6. A *hyperbole* is an intentional understatement of the facts.

_____ 7. *Malevolent* behavior is designed with the misfortune of others in mind.

_____ 8. A *heteronym* and an antonym are almost the same thing.

_____ 9. *Hypertension* is a desirable quality in bridge cable.

_____10. A scientific law is also known as a *hypothesis*.

_____11. *Hyperactive* children can be difficult to manage.

_____12. One normally thinks of a *malignancy* as something one could better do without.

SENTENCE FILL-IN

1. Since the words "roll" and "role" are pronounced the same way, they are

   _____.

2. A successful scientific experiment is likely to begin with a reasonable

   _____.

3. By the careful use of _____, the poet was able to inject considerable humor into his verse.

4. The words "tear" (as when we cry) and "tear" (as when we rip something up) are

   _____.

5. We are all _____ when we pretend unbending virtue.

6. Living in a great _____ metropolis offers almost unlimited opportunities for learning about different kinds of people.

7. Weary of charges of _____ in office, the mayor resigned.

8. _____ seems to have become the occupational ailment of the harried executive.

9. If we _____ our society, everyone will be pretty much the same.

10. The dastardly villain had _____ designs on the unsuspecting community.

11. _____ people often make those around them nervous as well.

12. The cancer specialist said that the patient's _____ may well have been caused by ingesting chemically treated foods.

MATCHING

____ 1. *mal*ignancy

____ 2. *hetero*geneous

____ 3. *mal*feasance

____ 4. *heter*onym

____ 5. *mal*evolent

____ 6. *homo*genize

____ 7. *hypo*thesis

____ 8. *hom*onym

____ 9. *hypo*critical

____ 10. *hyper*active

____ 11. *hyper*tension

____ 12. *hyper*bole

a. wishing bad things to happen to other people; showing ill will

b. an exaggeration of the literal facts

c. to make uniform throughout

d. high blood pressure

e. misconduct, especially by a person in public office

f. pretending to be more virtuous than one is

g. composed of elements or items which are unlike

h. a yet-to-be-proved assumption

i. a word with the same spelling as another, but with a different pronunciation and meaning

j. a word with the same pronunciation as another, but with different spelling and meaning

k. abnormally high-strung; unable to remain stationary

l. an evil or harmful growth or condition

SENTENCE COMPLETION

1. Chronic *hypertension* may eventually _____

_____

2. *Homonyms* do not have to be _____

_____

3. Few *malignancies* of this type are _____

_____

4. It was a *heterogeneous* coalition of _____

_____

5. Such *malevolent* sentiments are _____

_____

6. These *hyperactive* little creatures make _____

_____

7. Word games containing *heteronyms* can _____

_____

8. This continued *malfeasance* will almost certainly _____

_____

9. Isn't it a little *hypocritical* for a government employee to _____

_____

10. *Homogenized* milk has been _____

_____

11. Your *hypothesis* seems valid, but _____

_____

12. The *hyperbole* was not intended to _____

_____

Words with Prefixes (10)
Quality and Condition

PREFIXES

*1. *in-, ig-, il-; im-, ir-* (not): insane, ignore, illegal, immature, irreligious _____

_____

_____

2. *macro-* (large, great): macrobiotics _____

3. *micro-* (small, minute): microphone _____

4. *mis-* (bad, wrong, hatred): miscarriage _____

WORD LIST

1. *ig*noble (ig-NOW-bəl): possessing a low or base character
2. *il*legible (i-LEJ-ə-bəl): impossible to read or make out the meaning of
3. *il*licit (i-LIS-it): prohibited by law; illegal
4. *im*moderate (i-MAHD-ər-it): without reasonable restraint; excessive
5. *in*credible (in-KRED-ə-bəl): too unusual to be believed
6. *in*scrutable (in-SKRUW-tə-bəl): very difficult to understand; obscure or mysterious
7. *ir*rational (i-RASH-ə-nəl): lacking the power to think; senseless or absurd
8. *macro*cosm (MAK-rə-*kahz*-əm): the greater world or universe; a total system
9. *micro*cosm (MIY-krə-*kahz*-əm): a miniature model, as of the universe or a system
10. *micro*fiche (MIY-krə-*feesh*): a sheet of film containing reduced pages
11. *mis*construe (*mis*-kən-STRUW): to understand wrongly; to confuse
12. *mis*demeanor (*mis*-di-MEE-nər): a minor infraction of the law, less than a felony

---

a (f*a*t);   ay (f*a*te);   ah (f*a*r);   au (d*ou*bt);   ch (*ch*ur*ch*);   e (s*e*lf, c*a*re);   ee (*e*vening);   ə (*a*bout);   f (*f*lag, *ph*one);   hw (*wh*ile);   i (f*i*t);   iy (k*i*te);   ŋ (li*n*k, si*ng*);   o (*au*dio, c*o*rn);   ow (*o*pen);   oo (c*oo*k);   oi (*oi*l);   sh (*sh*oe, ambi*ti*on);   th (*th*ink);   u (*u*p, l*o*ve);   uw (*oo*ze);   yu (c*u*re);   yuw (*you*th, *u*nited);   zh (plea*s*ure)

TRUE-FALSE

_____ 1. Treason is a *misdemeanor*.

_____ 2. An *incredible* statement is very difficult to believe.

_____ 3. One is likely to find a *microfiche* file in the library.

_____ 4. *Illicit* activities are unlawful.

_____ 5. One can expect *ignoble* enterprises to be honorable.

_____ 6. The *macrocosm* of the universe may be greater than the human mind can perceive.

_____ 7. A *microcosm* may be thought of as a miniature universe.

_____ 8. To *misconstrue* is to perceive with clarity.

_____ 9. The *immoderate* use of foul language offends many people.

_____10. *Irrational* acts often defy a reasonable explanation.

_____11. *Inscrutable* people always lay their cards on the table.

_____12. *Illegible* handwriting is difficult to read.

SENTENCE FILL-IN

1. _____ consumption of almost anything that can be consumed may be harmful to one's health.

2. The death penalty for a _____ seems a little severe.

3. There is evidence that bombardment with microwaves can produce _____ behavior in many people.

4. The degree of reduction on sheets of _____ is not always the same.

5. The FBI has repeatedly been accused of _____ wiretapping.

6. Students are likely to be misled if they really believe that a college campus is a

   _____ of society at large.

7. The king's continued association with these _____ subversives belies his royal ancestry.

8. If you _____ my simplest instructions, what will you do with the more complex ones?

164

9. How _____ it is that the Russians, who pretend to run a people's state, refuse to allow freedom of speech.

10. The glib cynic called the universal _____ "God's playpen."

11. My doctor's handwriting was so _____ that the pharmacist couldn't read the prescription.

12. Marvin remained _____ to the end; we never knew what was bothering him.

MATCHING

_____ 1. *mis*demeanor

_____ 2. *ig*noble

_____ 3. *mis*construe

_____ 4. *il*legible

_____ 5. *micro*fiche

_____ 6. *il*licit

_____ 7. *micro*cosm

_____ 8. *im*moderate

_____ 9. *macro*cosm

_____ 10. *in*credible

_____ 11. *ir*rational

_____ 12. *in*scrutable

a. without reasonable restraint; excessive
b. a sheet of film containing reduced pages
c. a minor infraction of the law, less than a felony
d. lacking the power to think; senseless or absurd
e. very difficult to understand; obscure or mysterious
f. to understand wrongly; to confuse
g. impossible to read or make out the meaning of
h. possessing a low or base character
i. prohibited by law; illegal
j. the greater world or universe; a total system
k. too unusual to be believed
l. a miniature model, as of the universe or a system

SENTENCE COMPLETION

1. The modern business *macrocosm* includes _____

_____

2. An *immoderate* amount of _____

_____

Words with Suffixes (1)

SUFFIXES

1. *-acy, -cy* (N):   accuracy, infancy _____

2. *-ar* (A):   circular _____

3. *-ative* (A):   authoritative _____

4. *-ee* (N):   employee _____

5. *-fy, -efy, -ify* (V):   satisfy, liquefy, modify _____

6. *-ine* (A):   feminine _____

WORD LIST

1. absent*ee* (*ab*-sən-TEE):   one who is not present, as at an appointed time
2. bov*ine* (BOW-*viyn*):   slow (oxlike) in movement or thought; stupid
3. celiba*cy* (SEL-ə-bə-see):   abstinence from sex or marriage
4. demonstr*ative* (di-MAHN-strə-tiv):   inclined to show feelings and emotions openly
5. design*ee* (*dez*-ig-NEE):   a person who has been named or pointed out
6. fall*acy* (FAL-ə-see):   any mistake in the process of logical thought
7. line*ar* (LIN-ee-ər):   in a direct or logical sequence; on-line
8. pac*ify* (PAS-ə-*fiy*):   to make peaceful, tranquil, or calm
9. prist*ine* (PRIS-*teen*):   characteristic of earlier times and therefore less corrupt; pure, untouched
10. remuner*ative* (ri-MYUW-nə-*ray*-tiv):   offering the opportunity for ample profits
11. titul*ar* (TICH-ə-lər):   existing in name or title but without any real power or authority
12. vil*ify* (VIL-ə-*fiy*):   to try to make (someone) appear mean and evil; to slander

---

a (fat);   ay (fate);   ah (far);   au (doubt);   ch (church);   e (self, care);   ee (evening);   ə (about);   f (flag, phone);   hw (while);   i (fit);   iy (kite);   ŋ (link, sing);   o (audio, corn);   ow (open);   oo (cook);   oi (oil);   sh (shoe, ambition);   th (think);   u (up, love);   uw (ooze);   yu (cure);   yuw (youth, united);   zh (pleasure)

TRUE-FALSE

_____ 1. A person in a *titular* position has no title.

_____ 2. A *designee* is a person who has just been fired from his job.

_____ 3. A *bovine* creature is likely to be slow afoot.

_____ 4. A *fallacy* is likely to lead one to a false conclusion.

_____ 5. *Pristine* thoughts are likely to be pure and innocent.

_____ 6. *Demonstrative* people are usually very quiet and reserved.

_____ 7. *Linear* reasoning is logical and sequential.

_____ 8. A chronic *absentee* from the job is a dependable worker.

_____ 9. A *remunerative* enterprise is a profitable one.

_____10. *Celibacy* is likely to be practiced in a harem.

_____11. We usually try to *vilify* our best friends.

_____12. It is always a great temptation to *pacify* a crying child.

SENTENCE FILL-IN AND PART-OF-SPEECH IDENTIFICATION

_____ 1. By copious reading, you can develop your capacity to deal with

_____ thought.

_____ 2. Though we can _____ the stockholders' complaints with a dividend, we will not have improved the company's declining position.

_____ 3. The original owner's will stipulated that this area be maintained as a

_____ wilderness.

_____ 4. The more _____ members of the family wept openly.

_____ 5. Must we _____ everyone whose ideas don't happen to agree with what is popular at the moment?

_____ 6. As might be expected, all the _____ claimed not to have been notified of the meeting.

_____ 7. The _____ in your argument is that you incorrectly assumed the rest of the committee members would agree with you.

_____ 8. Only the _____ head of the department, Jarvis has no real authority.

_____ 9. Historically, Roman Catholic priests have taken a vow of _____.

_____ 10. Though the runner loped along with a _____ stride, he covered the course in pretty good time.

_____ 11. All the really _____ cases are handled by the full partners in the firm.

_____ 12. Baxter is the unofficial _____ for the new position as head of public relations.

MATCHING

_____ 1. vil*ify*

_____ 2. absent*ee*

_____ 3. titul*ar*

_____ 4. bov*ine*

_____ 5. remuner*ative*

_____ 6. celiba*cy*

_____ 7. prist*ine*

_____ 8. demonstr*ative*

_____ 9. pac*ify*

_____ 10. design*ee*

_____ 11. line*ar*

_____ 12. fall*acy*

a. any mistake in the process of logical thought
b. in a direct or logical sequence; on-line
c. slow (oxlike) in movement or thought; stupid
d. one who is not present, as at an appointed time
e. characteristic of earlier times and therefore less corrupt; pure, untouched
f. to make peaceful, tranquil, or calm
g. inclined to show feelings and emotions openly
h. to try to make (someone) appear mean and evil; to slander
i. offering the opportunity for ample profits
j. abstinence from sex or marriage
k. existing in name or title but without any real power or authority
l. a person who has been named or pointed out

SENTENCE COMPLETION

1. Too much time and money would be needed to *pacify* these _____

_____

2. Though this job is *remunerative* enough, it _____

_____

3. Enough little bits of information like this could *vilify* even _____

_____

4. Edmund's position as *titular* party leader does not accurately reflect his _____

_____

5. The practice of *celibacy* is no longer _____

_____

6. The imbecile's *bovine* attempts at thought were _____

_____

7. Such *pristine* beauty is seldom _____

_____

8. No one expected the *designee* for the position to _____

_____

9. The *linear* arrangement of _____

_____

10. Though an *absentee* for several weeks, the student _____

_____

11. Perhaps a less *demonstrative* presentation would _____

_____

12. It is always easier to spot a *fallacy* in _____

_____

Words with Suffixes (2)

SUFFIXES

1. *-ary* (A): temporary _____

2. *-ation* (N): starvation _____

3. *-ile* (A): hostile _____

4. *-ly* (A): fatherly _____

5. *-ment* (N): sediment _____

6. *-ure* (N): composure _____

WORD LIST

1. abomin*ation* (ə-*bahm*-ə-NAY-shən): anything outstandingly hateful and disgusting
2. culin*ary* (KYUW-lə-*ner*-ee): related to or used in the kitchen; suitable for cooking
3. detri*ment* (DE-trə-mənt): anything causing harm or injury; a disadvantage
4. disclos*ure* (dis-KLOW-zhər): an exposure, revelation, or explanation
5. doc*ile* (DAHS-əl): easily taught or managed
6. induce*ment* (in-DUWS-mənt): anything used to convince someone to do or believe something
7. port*ly* (PORT-lee): stout or heavy of build
8. primogenit*ure* (*priy*-mə-JEN-ə-chər): the practice of most of the inheritance going to the firstborn, especially the firstborn son
9. puer*ile* (PYUW-ər-əl): trivial and immature in a silly, childish way
10. reform*ation* (*ref*-ər-MAY-shən): a reorganizing or restructuring
11. sedent*ary* (SED-ən-*ter*-ee): inclined to sit or remain in one place; inactive
12. sur*ly* (SUR-lee): uncivil to the point of being threatening

---

a (f*a*t); ay (f*a*te); ah (f*a*r); au (d*ou*bt); ch (*ch*ur*ch*); e (s*e*lf, c*a*re); ee (*e*vening); ə (*a*bout); f (*f*lag, *ph*one); hw (*wh*ile); i (f*i*t); iy (k*i*te); ŋ (li*nk*, si*ng*); o (*au*dio, c*or*n); ow (*o*pen); oo (c*oo*k); oi (*oi*l); sh (*sh*oe, ambi*ti*on); th (*th*ink); u (*u*p, l*o*ve); uw (*oo*ze); yu (c*u*re); yuw (*you*th, *u*nited); zh (plea*s*ure)

TRUE-FALSE

_____ 1. Something that is done to your *detriment* will most likely do you some harm.

_____ 2. *Portly* people usually look as if they need a good meal.

_____ 3. A *puerile* response to criticism will be mature and enlightened.

_____ 4. A *disclosure* can reveal what was not known before.

_____ 5. The result of a *reformation* can be a fresh start.

_____ 6. Professional athletes normally lead very *sedentary* lives.

_____ 7. *Primogeniture* involves an equal distribution of an estate among its heirs.

_____ 8. *Surly* behavior is unlikely to assist in the formation of friendships.

_____ 9. An *abomination* is anything greatly prized.

_____10. Something that is good to eat might be called a *culinary* delight.

_____11. A *docile* child is one who refuses instruction.

_____12. To the coward, the threat of physical violence can be a persuasive *inducement*.

SENTENCE FILL-IN AND PART-OF-SPEECH IDENTIFICATION

_____ 1. Twenty years of _____ living has left Reginald in poor physical condition.

_____ 2. Though _____ enough today, that old lion was once a ferocious beast.

_____ 3. Nathan's _____ antics on the tennis court have won him the nickname of "Nasty."

_____ 4. Once slender and athletic, Gifford has become a _____ middle-aged businessman.

_____ 5. A complete _____ of the government was begun after the revolution.

_____ 6. It was a substantial financial _____ that seemed to reduce the risks of the assignment.

_____ 7. Public _____ of the senator's malfeasance cost him his place on his party's ticket.

_____ 8. One does not expect such _____ opinions from a person with such a mature reputation.

_____ 9. Your accepting a campaign contribution from the Mafia will ultimately prove a

_____ to your career.

_____10. The little duchy's tradition of _____ gives most of the family's wealth to the oldest son.

_____11. The modern disposition almost to worship objects symbolic of the so-called good

life has become a moral _____.

_____12. My great-grandmother was a master of the _____ arts, though she had only the simplest implements to work with.

MATCHING

_____ 1. sur*ly*

_____ 2. culin*ary*

_____ 3. sedent*ary*

_____ 4. abomin*ation*

_____ 5. puer*ile*

_____ 6. detri*ment*

_____ 7. primogenit*ure*

_____ 8. disclos*ure*

_____ 9. port*ly*

_____10. induce*ment*

_____11. doc*ile*

_____12. reform*ation*

a. inclined to sit or remain in one place; inactive
b. anything used to convince someone to do or believe something
c. an exposure, revelation, or explanation
d. related to or used in the kitchen; suitable for cooking
e. uncivil to the point of being threatening
f. trivial and immature in a silly, childish way
g. anything outstandingly hateful and disgusting
h. anything causing harm or injury; a disadvantage
i. stout or heavy of build
j. a reorganizing or restructuring
k. easily taught or managed
l. the practice of most of the inheritance going to the firstborn, especially the firstborn son

SENTENCE COMPLETION

1. A more complete *disclosure* of the facts will _____

_____

2. *Primogeniture* has long since _____

_____

185

3. It is no *detriment* to you that _____

_____

4. Many chefs attribute their *culinary* skills to _____

_____

5. A more concrete *inducement* would _____

_____

6. Your *puerile* behavior at _____

_____

7. Such cultural *abominations* as _____

_____

8. Although he was somewhat *portly,* Ashley could _____

_____

9. Tony is sometimes *surly* when he first comes to the office, but he _____

_____

10. Made *docile* by the drug, Alexander _____

_____

11. A *reformation* of manners might _____

_____

12. Such *sedentary* employment will _____

_____

Words with Suffixes (3)

SUFFIXES

1. *-age* (N): postage _____

2. *-ery, -ary* (N): slavery, missionary _____

3. *-ical* (A): historical _____

4. *-ing* (A): fulfilling _____

5. *-istic* (A): optimistic _____

6. *-ize* (V): realize _____

WORD LIST

1. cauter*ize* (KO-tə-*riyz*): to burn or sear, as with an iron or needle
2. cut*lery* (KUT-lər-ee): various implements used for cutting, especially in the preparation of food
3. debilitat*ing* (di-BIL-ə-*tay*-tiŋ): making weak, feeble, or unable to function
4. galvan*ize* (GAL-və-*niyz*): to startle (electrically) into action; to excite
5. gran*ary* (GRAN-ər-ee): a place where grains are grown or stored
6. inhibit*ing* (in-HIB-ə-tiŋ): restraining or holding back
7. inim*ical* (in-IM-i-kəl): like an enemy; hostile and unfriendly
8. nihil*istic* (*niy*-əl-IS-tik): related generally to the belief that there is no meaning or purpose to life
9. plural*istic* (*ploor*-əl-IS-tik): characteristic of a society with several bases of political and social power
10. port*age* (POR-tij): the act of carrying anything, as a boat overland
11. rhetor*ical* (ri-TOR-i-kəl): related to the (showy) use of the various devices of effective writing or speech
12. rough*age* (RUF-ij): coarse materials used as food or fodder

---

a (f*a*t); ay (f*a*te); ah (f*a*r); au (d*o*ubt); ch (*church*); e (s*e*lf, c*a*re); ee (*e*vening); ə (*a*bout); f (*f*lag, *ph*one); hw (*wh*ile); i (f*i*t); iy (k*i*te); ŋ (li*n*k, si*ng*); o (*au*dio, c*or*n); ow (*o*pen); oo (c*oo*k); oi (*oi*l); sh (*sh*oe, ambi*ti*on); th (*th*ink); u (*u*p, l*o*ve); uw (*oo*ze); yu (c*u*re); yuw (*you*th, *u*nited); zh (plea*s*ure)

TRUE-FALSE

_____ 1. *Rhetorical* skills are important to professional writers.

_____ 2. Conditions *inimical* to learning are characteristic of the best schools.

_____ 3. A *nihilistic* view of life places great faith in human institutions.

_____ 4. Horses and cows live almost exclusively on *roughage*.

_____ 5. To *galvanize* is to put to sleep with soft music.

_____ 6. To *cauterize* is to put into a hard freeze.

_____ 7. A *portage* is a heavy broth containing beef stock.

_____ 8. A set of *cutlery* may include several sharp knives.

_____ 9. *Debilitating* illnesses usually leave their victims stronger and more vigorous than ever.

_____10. A *granary* is a place designed for taming birds.

_____11. A *pluralistic* economy would be less likely to collapse than an economy based on the production of a single product.

_____12. Anything *inhibiting* growth is likely to produce greater size.

SENTENCE FILL-IN AND PART-OF-SPEECH IDENTIFICATION

_____ 1. A _____ of five miles was necessary to get from one fork of the river to another.

_____ 2. Current dietary theory has it that a moderate amount of _____ in one's diet is healthful.

_____ 3. It would be very difficult for a single institution to control a country as

_____ as ours.

_____ 4. Constant failure can have a _____ effect on almost anyone.

_____ 5. Few doctrines have been more _____ to the development of democratic institutions than that of the existence of a natural aristocracy.

_____ 6. An expert at every _____ technique in the book, Constance is a very difficult person to argue with.

_____ 7. Squire Allworthy gave his cook an expensive set of _____ for her birthday.

188

_____ 8. If we do not _____ this wound at once, an infection is likely to occur.

_____ 9. Do you think another catastrophe like Pearl Harbor would _____ this nation into unified action?

_____10. The Midwest is often called the great American _____.

_____11. The _____ band of terrorists wanted only to destroy everything they did not approve of.

_____12. Laws _____ to individual freedom do not protect us from anyone, much less from ourselves.

MATCHING

_____ 1. rough*age*

_____ 2. cauter*ize*

_____ 3. rhetor*ical*

_____ 4. cut*lery*

_____ 5. galvan*ize*

_____ 6. debilitat*ing*

_____ 7. port*age*

_____ 8. gran*ary*

_____ 9. plural*istic*

_____10. inhibit*ing*

_____11. nihil*istic*

_____12. inim*ical*

a. to startle (electrically) into action; to excite
b. like an enemy; hostile and unfriendly
c. a place where grains are grown or stored
d. coarse materials used as food or fodder
e. the act of carrying anything, as a boat overland
f. various implements used for cutting, especially in the preparation of food
g. to burn or sear, as with an iron or needle
h. related to the (showy) use of the various devices of effective writing or speech
i. making weak, feeble, or unable to function
j. related generally to the belief that there is no meaning or purpose to life
k. characteristic of a society with several bases of political and social power
l. restraining or holding back

SENTENCE COMPLETION

1. Few things are more socially *inhibiting* than _____

_____

2. The *cutlery* salesperson left a _____

_____

3. By the clever use of *rhetorical* devices, one can _____

4. How can we *cauterize* such a _____

5. Perhaps we can *galvanize* the forces by _____

6. Forces *inimical* to our cause are _____

7. Typical items of dietary *roughage* include _____

8. Such *nihilistic* arguments hardly _____

9. A *debilitating* injury _____

10. Even in the most *pluralistic* of societies, _____

11. The *portage* fee was almost _____

12. A series of *granary* fires resulted in _____

Words with Suffixes (4)

SUFFIXES

1. *-acity* (N): loquacity _____

2. *-al, -ial* (A): natural, jovial _____

3. *-eer, -ier* (N): mountaineer, cashier _____

4. *-ility* (N): imbecility _____

5. *-less* (A): colorless _____

6. *-ose* (A): verbose _____

WORD LIST

1. ban*al* (BAY-nəl): without freshness or originality; stale and commonplace
2. civ*ility* (sə-VIL-ə-tee): politeness; a courteous act or statement
3. comat*ose* (KAHM-ə-*tows*): almost unconscious; in a stupor
4. convivi*al* (kən-VIV-ee-əl): fond of feasting, drinking, and good company; festive
5. finan*cier* (*fin*-ən-SEER): one clever (expert) at handling stocks, bonds, investments, and other money matters
6. fut*ility* (fyuw-TIL-ə-tee): condition of hopelessness or uselessness
7. hap*less* (HAP-lis): without much luck; unfortunate, as if by nature
8. joc*ose* (jow-KOWS): jokingly playful or humorous
9. profit*eer* (*prahf*-ə-TEER): one who takes advantage of a market shortage to charge very high prices
10. relent*less* (ri-LENT-lis): persistent; never letting up
11. ten*acity* (tə-NAS-ə-tee): the ability to hold on firmly, as to beliefs or goals
12. ver*acity* (və-RAS-ə-tee): precision in sticking to the truth

---

a (fat);   ay (fate);   ah (far);   au (doubt);   ch (church);   e (self, care);   ee (evening);   ə (about);   f (flag, phone);   hw (while);   i (fit);   iy (kite);   ŋ (link, sing);   o (audio, corn);   ow (open);   oo (cook);   oi (oil);   sh (shoe, ambition);   th (think);   u (up, love);   uw (ooze);   yu (cure);   yuw (youth, united);   zh (pleasure)

TRUE-FALSE

_____ 1. *Banal* remarks are clever and witty.

_____ 2. A *relentless* adversary is one who never stops opposing you.

_____ 3. *Tenacity* of purpose is likely to suggest a certain strength of character.

_____ 4. *Futility* usually breeds optimism.

_____ 5. Vulgarity in public is an example of *civility*.

_____ 6. To speak with *veracity* is to tell the truth.

_____ 7. A *financier* is likely to be much occupied with money.

_____ 8. A *comatose* state may be induced by a drug.

_____ 9. A *convivial* party is one at which everyone refuses to mingle with others.

_____10. *Hapless* people should stay away from racetracks.

_____11. *Jocose* people are usually moody and sarcastic.

_____12. A *profiteer* is a businessperson with a strong social conscience.

SENTENCE FILL-IN AND PART-OF-SPEECH IDENTIFICATION

_____ 1. As it turned out, pleasantly enough, the class reunion was a _____ affair.

_____ 2. A very _____ fellow, Hodge always has a string of jokes on the tip of his tongue.

_____ 3. Often only the very finest of lines separates the unscrupulous _____ from the astute speculator.

_____ 4. Are you really questioning the _____ of this eminent scholar's research?

_____ 5. Though the civil rights movement may not be dead, it is unquestionably

_____.

_____ 6. When the _____ of our enterprise became obvious to us, we gave up and went home.

_____ 7. Filled with one _____ observation after another, the essay was commonplace in the extreme.

_____ 8. With _____ courage, the infantrymen continued the attack day after day.

192

_____ 9. A seemingly congenital _____ will not allow Truman to give up on any project once he starts it.

_____ 10. As a result of the current energy situation, the Arab _____ is the new face in international investment.

_____ 11. This _____ character seems to manufacture bad luck everywhere he goes.

_____ 12. A general _____ among the citizens made the village a pleasant place to live.

MATCHING

_____ 1. ver*acity*

_____ 2. ban*al*

_____ 3. ten*acity*

_____ 4. civ*ility*

_____ 5. relent*less*

_____ 6. coma*tose*

_____ 7. profit*eer*

_____ 8. conviv*ial*

_____ 9. joc*ose*

_____ 10. financ*ier*

_____ 11. hap*less*

_____ 12. fut*ility*

a. without much luck; unfortunate, as if by nature
b. one clever (expert) at handling stocks, bonds, investments, and other money matters
c. persistent; never letting up
d. the ability to hold on firmly, as to beliefs or goals
e. precision in sticking to the truth
f. without freshness or originality; stale and commonplace
g. politeness; a courteous act or statement
h. almost unconscious; in a stupor
i. fond of feasting, drinking, and good company; festive
j. condition of hopelessness or uselessness
k. one who takes advantage of a market shortage to charge very high prices
l. jokingly playful or humorous

SENTENCE COMPLETION

1. As an exercise in *futility,* you might try your hand at _____

_____

2. With the *tenacity* of a snapping turtle, Beatrice _____

_____

3. A more experienced *financier* would never have _____

_____

4. A *hapless* victim of circumstances, Montgomery _____

_____

5. The governor has waged a *relentless* campaign to _____

_____

6. Your *jocose* manner was inappropriate for _____

_____

7. The *veracity* of the ambassador's statements leaves _____

_____

8. A *profiteer* in adolescent clothing fads, Edwin _____

_____

9. A higher level of *civility* might _____

_____

10. Rendered *comatose* by a _____

_____

11. A *convivial* collection of drunks _____

_____

12. Such *banal* attempts at scholarship are _____

_____

Words with Suffixes (5)

SUFFIXES

1. *-able, -ible* (A): portable, horrible _____

2. *-escent* (A): phosphorescent _____

3. *-esque* (A): picturesque _____

4. *-ion* (N): fusion _____

5. *-ish* (V): furnish _____

6. *-ity* (N): clarity _____

WORD LIST

1. allus*ion* (ə-LUW-zhən): a passing, casual, or indirect mention of something
2. burl*esque* (bər-LESK): done in a mockingly or ludicrously imitating manner
3. contrit*ion* (kən-TRISH-ən): the feeling of sorrow and remorse for having done wrong
4. efferv*escent* (ef-ər-VES-ənt): high-spirited; bubbling over
5. flour*ish* (FLUR-ish): to grow and prosper; to blossom and become successful
6. fluor*escent* (floo-RES-ənt): giving off light, as mercury vapor in a tube
7. intang*ible* (in-TAN-jə-bəl): that which cannot be touched, seen, or easily defined
8. laud*able* (LO-də-bəl): worthy of praise; commendable
9. longev*ity* (lahn-JEV-ə-tee): the length of life, especially a long life
10. par*ity* (PAR-ə-tee): equality or resemblance of value, rank, or power
11. refurb*ish* (ri-FUR-bish): to freshen up and make like new again
12. statu*esque* (*stach*-oo-WESK): possessing a well-proportioned and graceful dignity

TRUE-FALSE

_____ 1. The *longevity* of a turtle extends beyond that of a hummingbird.

_____ 2. To *flourish* is to become old and decayed.

---

a (f*a*t); ay (f*a*te); ah (f*a*r); au (d*ou*bt); ch (*ch*urch); e (s*e*lf, c*a*re); ee (*e*vening); ə (*a*bout); f (*f*lag, *ph*one); hw (*wh*ile); i (f*i*t); iy (k*i*te); ŋ (li*nk*, si*ng*); o (*au*dio, c*o*rn); ow (*o*pen); oo (c*oo*k); oi (*oi*l); sh (*sh*oe, ambi*ti*on); th (*th*ink); u (*u*p, l*o*ve); uw (*oo*ze); yu (c*u*re); yuw (*y*outh, *u*nited); zh (plea*s*ure)

_____ 3. An automobile is an *intangible* object.

_____ 4. *Burlesque* imitations should always be taken very seriously.

_____ 5. Short, plump people are usually thought of as *statuesque*.

_____ 6. An *allusion* is a blatant statement of fact.

_____ 7. An *effervescent* creature is one that glows in the dark.

_____ 8. A feeling of *contrition* assumes wrongdoing.

_____ 9. It has been proved that there is an absolute *parity* of intelligence among all people on earth.

_____10. Anything *fluorescent* gives off light.

_____11. *Laudable* activities are worthy of praise.

_____12. To *refurbish* an old car is to sell it for junk.

SENTENCE FILL-IN AND PART-OF-SPEECH IDENTIFICATION

_____ 1. The _____ bulb buzzed and crackled before exploding.

_____ 2. Few actions are more _____ than for young people to look after their aging parents.

_____ 3. Edwin's _____ antics often annoy people who take themselves seriously.

_____ 4. A few buckets of paint and some minor repairs should _____ the old place well enough.

_____ 5. Though our new model is extremely _____, she can't seem to hold still for more than a few minutes at a time.

_____ 6. No one could blame the old man for being proud of his health and

_____ .

_____ 7. A single alert student caught the professor's _____ to Shakespeare's *Julius Caesar*.

_____ 8. The aging actor said that the American theater will _____ in spite of television.

_____ 9. It is always a little sad to see the _____ qualities of youth fizzle out under the pressure of life's experiences.

_____10. The union was demanding wage _____ for its members all across the country.

_____ 11. The accused person's pretended _____ fooled no one, including the judge.

_____ 12. The critics agreed that the young actress possessed an _____ quality that made her performance effective.

MATCHING

_____ 1. stat*uesque*

_____ 2. allus*ion*

_____ 3. refurb*ish*

_____ 4. burl*esque*

_____ 5. par*ity*

_____ 6. contrit*ion*

_____ 7. longev*ity*

_____ 8. efferv*escent*

_____ 9. laud*able*

_____ 10. flour*ish*

_____ 11. intang*ible*

_____ 12. fluor*escent*

a. to grow and prosper; to blossom and become successful
b. the feeling of sorrow and remorse for having done wrong
c. the length of life, especially a long life
d. worthy of praise; commendable
e. a passing, casual, or indirect mention of something
f. done in a mockingly or ludicrously imitating manner
g. high-spirited; bubbling over
h. to freshen up and make like new again
i. equality or resemblance of value, rank, or power
j. giving off light, as mercury vapor in a tube
k. possessing a well-proportioned and graceful dignity
l. that which cannot be touched, seen, or easily defined

SENTENCE COMPLETION

1. I doubt that the *longevity* of this idea will _____

_____

2. What a *statuesque* appearance the _____

_____

3. Why bother to *refurbish* such _____

_____

4. The child's *effervescent* smile _____

_____

5. Except for the young soldier's *vigilance* at his post, we _____

_____

6. Such *benevolent* thoughts seldom _____

_____

7. *Procrastinate* long enough and _____

_____

8. How can we *alleviate* the pressure on _____

_____

9. The *plentitude* of the industrialized nations _____

_____

10. Frequently, the most *gainful* enterprises require _____

_____

11. *Doleful* days followed the _____

_____

12. A *multitude* of problems faced _____

_____

Self-scoring Posttest

MULTIPLE CHOICE

Place the letter of the best answer in the blank space.

_____ 1. An *animated* discussion is likely to be
  a. boring
  b. very academic
  c. spirited
  d. without logic

_____ 2. An *armistice* is a
  a. pitched battle
  b. musical instrument
  c. sleeve band
  d. temporary peace

_____ 3. *Bellicose* people are often
  a. absentminded
  b. quarrelsome
  c. musically inclined
  d. peacemakers

_____ 4. *Carnage* is likely to involve
  a. much bloodshed
  b. a good time for all
  c. diplomatic agreements
  d. urbanization

_____ 5. A *concise* statement is likely to be
  a. lengthy
  b. flowery
  c. to the point
  d. untruthful

_____ 6. Anything that is *recurrent*
  a. insults someone
  b. raises unanswered questions
  c. causes damage
  d. happens again and again

_____ 7. A *definitive* statement must be
  a. ambiguous
  b. ironical
  c. popular
  d. authoritative

_____ 8. A *fortuitous* event
  a. happens by chance
  b. requires planning
  c. arouses jealousy
  d. is of artistic significance

_____ 9. To *confound* is to
  a. mispronounce
  b. bewilder
  c. compliment
  d. elaborate upon

_____ 10. A *hostelry* is
  a. a thief
  b. a roadside park
  c. a bloody battle
  d. an inn

_____ 11. A *libertarian* is
  a. an immoral person
  b. a great reader of novels
  c. one who believes in equal freedom for all
  d. an atheist

_____ 12. A *pellucid* explanation is
  a. very clear and understandable
  b. unnecessarily complex
  c. of questionable authenticity
  d. circumlocutory

13. To *commemorate* is to
    a. let pass into oblivion
    b. remember with ceremony
    c. destroy altogether
    d. make appear more important

14. A *commodious* habitat is likely to be
    a. damp
    b. very small
    c. comfortable
    d. infested with insects

15. A *patrician* appearance suggests
    a. villainy
    b. poverty
    c. nobleness
    d. obesity

16. An *imposition* is a
    a. proposition
    b. burden
    c. distortion
    d. tricky question

17. A *facsimile* is a
    a. romantic poem
    b. very close copy
    c. dark shade of blue
    d. factual statement

18. A *terrarium* is likely to contain
    a. tropical fish
    b. sea birds
    c. water colors
    d. plants

19. A *tortuous* explanation is likely to be
    a. enjoyable for everyone
    b. highly profitable
    c. needlessly devious
    d. educational

20. *Invidious* remarks are generally intended to
    a. arouse envy
    b. tranquilize
    c. mislead
    d. infatuate

21. *Symbiotic* relationships are always
    a. sexual
    b. introverted
    c. mutually beneficial
    d. exclusively economic

22. To *synchronize* is to
    a. attack openly
    b. debate at length
    c. alter the facts
    d. match up in time

23. *Dogmatic* assertions are made
    a. only after careful research
    b. without proof.
    c. only by pet owners
    d. for the good of others

24. *Monolithic* organizations are
    a. unyielding
    b. amorphous
    c. thoroughly democratic
    d. politically liberal

25. A *neologism* is a
    a. short philosophical statement
    b. new word
    c. visiting foreign dignitary
    d. patriotic song

26. A *synopsis* is a
    a. waterfowl
    b. stockbroker
    c. deductive argument
    d. summary

27. *Sophomoric* attitudes are
    a. immature
    b. brilliant
    c. occult
    d. psychedelic

28. *Theology* is the study of
    a. balloons
    b. God
    c. physics
    d. communications

29. An *attenuated* appearance suggests
   a. vitality
   b. weak moral character
   c. feebleness
   d. a desire to learn

30. *Antediluvian* ideas are
   a. of questionable authenticity
   b. old-fashioned
   c. paternalistic
   d. contemporary

31. *Coeval* forces must
   a. be evil
   b. possess equal power
   c. produce results
   d. exist at the same time

32. *Efficacious* results are
   a. to be greatly feared
   b. exactly those desired
   c. completely unexpected
   d. of questionable value

33. An *imminent* event is
   a. very important
   b. misrepresented in the press
   c. of consequence to no one
   d. likely to happen at any moment

34. An *oblique* lesson is likely to be
   a. of a most blatant nature
   b. indirectly learned
   c. not worth knowing
   d. entirely academic

35. To *transpose* is to
   a. reverse
   b. arrange logically
   c. confuse the meaning
   d. shorten

36. To be *disenchanted* is to be
   a. pleasantly surprised
   b. amoral
   c. disappointed with
   d. in favor of

37. *Malevolent* impulses
   a. are usually pleasant
   b. cause one to wish misfortune on others
   c. arise from innate feelings of brotherhood
   d. are childlike

38. An *incredible* event is
   a. unimportant
   b. historical
   c. unbelievable
   d. frightening

39. That which is *nonpareil* is
   a. ordinary
   b. inferior
   c. lifelike
   d. unmatched

40. A *tripartite* proposal includes
   a. three distinct items
   b. nothing new
   c. only tried and tested suggestions
   d. support from both major political parties

41. A *fallacy* is an
   a. antiquated idea
   b. ugly mask
   c. error in logic
   d. old tale

42. *Docile* creatures are
   a. inclined to fight
   b. easily managed
   c. impossible to teach
   d. often retarded

43. *Debilitating* experiences often
   a. enrich
   b. ennoble
   c. enliven
   d. enfeeble

44. *Convivial* people are likely to be
   a. friendly
   b. relentless
   c. comatose
   d. antisocial

_____ 45. To *refurbish* is to
    a. punish severely
    b. make like new
    c. spoil
    d. cross-examine

_____ 46. An *allusion* is
    a. a figment of the imagination
    b. a serious wound
    c. an indirect reference
    d. an equal amount

_____ 47. An *apprehensive* feeling includes
    a. optimism
    b. anxiety
    c. suppression
    d. malice

_____ 48. A *muted* sound is
    a. soft
    b. openly effeminate
    c. carelessly inappropriate
    d. tasteless

_____ 49. *Fulsome* praise is likely to be
    a. deserved
    b. given from the heart
    c. appropriate
    d. in questionable taste

_____ 50. A *gainful* enterprise is likely to be
    a. profitable
    b. illicit
    c. immoral
    d. without benefit to anyone

Answers: 1–c, 2–d, 3–b, 4–a, 5–c, 6–d, 7–d, 8–a, 9–b, 10–d, 11–c, 12–a, 13–b, 14–c, 15–c, 16–b, 17–b, 18–d, 19–c, 20–a, 21–c, 22–d, 23–b, 24–a, 25–b, 26–d, 27–a, 28–b, 29–c, 30–b, 31–d, 32–b, 33–d, 34–b, 35–a, 36–c, 37–b, 38–c, 39–d, 40–a, 41–c, 42–b, 43–d, 44–a, 45–b, 46–c, 47–b, 48–a, 49–d, 50–a

MULTIPLE CHOICE

Place the letter of the best answer in the bla

_____ 1. To *impeach* is to
   a. call in question
   b. throw out of office
   c. threaten
   d. flatter

_____ 2. *Ubiquitous* people are often
   a. lazy
   b. very religious
   c. easily angered
   d. in the way

_____ 3. We are most likely to suffer
   from *mal de mer*
   a. as infants
   b. after eating
   c. on a ship
   d. when unable to sleep

_____ 4. An *Elysian* state of mind is
   likely to be
   a. confusing
   b. blissful
   c. unstable
   d. moribund

_____ 5. To *raze* is to
   a. flatter
   b. level to the ground
   c. tease
   d. enrich the texture of

_____ 6. A *cul-de-sac* is a
   a. flower garden
   b. one-way street
   c. paper bag
   d. blind alley

PART TWO

WORD TYPES

Part Two of *Contemporary Vocabulary* includes chapters dealing with action words, descriptive words, words from names, and foreign expressions commonly used in good written English. All of these are important for anyone wishing to develop a fuller vocabulary. You have already seen examples of each in the chapters of Part One, but here the emphasis is shifted to the individual word types.

Before beginning these chapters, you may want to work through the self-scoring pretest, which will give you an idea of the variety of words you will be dealing with in this part of the book. The answers follow the test. Then, when you have completed Part Two, you can work through the posttest at the end of the book.

_____ 12. To *inveigle* is to
   a. go backward
   b. cover with decorations
   c. cleverly deceive
   d. cause to happen

_____ 13. A *stentorian* sound is
   a. melodic
   b. faint
   c. discordant
   d. loud

_____ 14. A *déjeuner* is a
   a. late breakfast
   b. railroad coach
   c. small booklet
   d. white wine

_____ 15. A *Wunderkind* is a
   a. European tobacco
   b. mystical religion
   c. complex question
   d. child prodigy

_____ 16. A *precipitous* decline occurs
   a. regularly
   b. over a period of time
   c. quickly
   d. only during the winter

_____ 17. To *mesmerize* is to
   a. take advantage of
   b. fascinate
   c. mock
   d. run away and hide

_____ 18. A *sagacious* person is likely to be
   a. senile
   b. perceptive
   c. untrustworthy
   d. in poor health

_____ 19. To *fructify* is to
   a. load down
   b. make fruitful
   c. claim falsely
   d. praise extravagantly

_____ 20. *Pro patria* statements are likely to sound
   a. patriotic
   b. confusing
   c. entertaining
   d. counterproductive

_____ 21. A *solon* is a
   a. saloon
   b. hunter
   c. lawmaker
   d. salon

_____ 22. *Micawberish* people are usually
   a. optimistic
   b. moody
   c. pessimistic
   d. apathetic

_____ 23. A *macadamized* road is
   a. crooked
   b. narrow
   c. paved
   d. unused

_____ 24. *Derisive* laughter can be
   a. contagious
   b. uplifting
   c. scornful
   d. instructive

_____ 25. A *cri de coeur* is
   a. a bowl of thick soup
   b. an impassioned cry
   c. a lifelong enemy
   d. an object of art

_____ 26. A *sobriquet* is a
   a. collection of flowers
   b. drunkard
   c. challenge to fight
   d. nickname

_____ 27. To *belie* is to
   a. picture falsely
   b. conclude illogically
   c. agree with
   d. disgrace in public

_____ 28. A *gaunt* appearance suggests
   a. robustness
   b. poor health
   c. wealth
   d. credibility

_____ 29. To *defray* is to
   a. start a fight
   b. make more lively
   c. provide for payment
   d. accuse of a crime

30. An *insouciant* manner is usually
    a. tense
    b. unbothered
    c. matter-of-fact
    d. belligerent

31. To *implement* is to
    a. pervert
    b. make amends for
    c. carry out
    d. attack

32. An *indelible* impression is
    a. nondescript
    b. elusive
    c. morbid
    d. permanent

33. A *fait accompli* is
    a. the latest cry
    b. the highest achievement
    c. an accomplished fact
    d. an official statement

34. To *lampoon* is to
    a. support
    b. ridicule
    c. imitate
    d. spear

35. A *tenuous* argument is likely to be
    a. flimsy
    b. emotional
    c. logical
    d. tripartite

36. A *harpy* is likely to be
    a. greedy
    b. cherubic
    c. stylish
    d. beautiful

37. A *bel-esprit* is a person of
    a. broad experience
    b. clever wit
    c. impeccable taste
    d. limited means

38. *Tawdry* jewelry is
    a. expensive
    b. customized
    c. usually rented
    d. showy

39. A *maverick* is a
    a. religious group
    b. wicked woman
    c. loner
    d. political prisoner

40. To *proscribe* is to
    a. admit defeat
    b. predict the future
    c. denounce
    d. condone

41. A *quisling* is a
    a. waterfowl
    b. fallacy
    c. patriot
    d. traitor

42. To *fathom* is to
    a. change the color of
    b. approach cautiously
    c. get to the bottom of
    d. eat greedily

43. To *promulgate* is to
    a. make widely known
    b. struggle against odds
    c. become inflexible
    d. make amends for

44. A *cogent* remark is likely to be
    a. confusing
    b. vulgar
    c. bizarre
    d. convincing

45. A *gaffe* is a
    a. nervous tic
    b. brilliant remark
    c. public blunder
    d. faded painting

46. *Icarian* boldness is likely to be
    a. foolish
    b. courageous
    c. long lasting
    d. intimidating

47. A *lothario* is
    a. an actor
    b. a lover
    c. an orator
    d. a wanderer

48. A *Sisyphean* enterprise requires
    a. large capital investment
    b. enormous expertise
    c. almost endless toil
    d. clever deception

49. A *lilliputian* point of view is likely to be
    a. perceptive
    b. practical
    c. pretentious
    d. petty

50. A *couturier* makes
    a. trouble
    b. predictions
    c. clothes
    d. furniture

Answers: 1–a, 2–d, 3–c, 4–b, 5–b, 6–d, 7–c, 8–a, 9–d, 10–d, 11–b, 12–c, 13–d, 14–a, 15–d, 16–c, 17–b, 18–b, 19–b, 20–a, 21–c, 22–a, 23–c, 24–c, 25–b, 26–d, 27–a, 28–b, 29–c, 30–b, 31–c, 32–d, 33–c, 34–b, 35–a, 36–a, 37–b, 38–d, 39–c, 40–c, 41–d, 42–c, 43–a, 44–d, 45–c, 46–a, 47–b, 48–c, 49–d, 50–c

Chapter 5

Action Words

Action words are verbs, and verbs are the principal words that give sentences movement and vitality. It is important that you have a good selection of verbs at your disposal when writing; otherwise your sentences are likely to be cluttered with an excessive number of "be" verbs and prepositional phrases. This clutter results in such limp sentences as those that follow. Notice how each is improved by the use of an action word:

limp: The committee members finally agreed with each other about what to do.

improved: The committee members finally *concurred* on what to do.

limp: It took John only a few weeks to become used to his new job.

improved: John *acclimated* himself to his new job in only a few weeks.

limp: Is it possible for me to convince you not to do this?

improved: Can I *dissuade* you from doing this?

limp: The speaker took back what he had said at first.

improved: The speaker *recanted* his earlier statements.

limp: For eight hours every day Arthur is at his studies.

improved: Arthur *immerses* himself in his studies eight hours daily.

limp: We should pass this information out to all of our branch managers immediately.

improved: We should *disseminate* this information among our branch managers immediately.

limp: Is there any way to get this program started and keep it moving?
improved: Is there any way to *implement* this program?

limp: Jimmy has always thought a very great deal of his uncle.
improved: Jimmy *reveres* his uncle.

limp: You will not make the voters think any more of you by doing this.
improved: You will not *enhance* your position with the voters by doing this.

limp: Conditions are such that it is time to cut back on all possible expenditures.
improved: Conditions *dictate* that we *retrench* all possible expenditures.

After the initial word lists that give pronunciations and definitions, the sequences in this chapter include two exercises—a sentence-completion exercise and a crisscross puzzle. Since crisscross puzzles may be new to you, take time to notice that the "across" words begin at the top and move steadily down. The "down" words, on the other hand, begin at the left and move to the right. The numbers for the "across" words are in the upper left of the numbered squares, and the numbers for the "down" words are in the upper right of the numbered squares. A square with two numbers begins both an "across" word and a "down" word.

Action Words (1)

WORD LIST

1. chide (CHIYD): to scold in a mild manner
2. condescend (*kahn*-də-SEND): to reduce oneself to a lower level; to patronize those of lower rank
3. deplore (di-PLOR): to regret very strongly
4. devise (di-VIYZ): to think up or contrive
5. distill (dis-TIL): to concentrate, purify, or refine
6. elicit (i-LIS-it): to draw out or cause to happen
7. espouse (i-SPAUZ): to advocate, as a cause or movement
8. fathom (FAT͡H-əm): to (try to) get to the bottom of
9. immerse (i-MURS): to plunge deeply into
10. impugn (im-PYUWN): to call into question by means of logical argument
11. incur (in-KUR): to bring upon oneself
12. intimate (IN-tə-*mayt*): to suggest or make known indirectly
13. pique (PEEK): to offend the pride of
14. proctor (PRAHK-tər): to supervise or monitor
15. proscribe (prow-SKRIYB): to denounce, banish, or condemn

SENTENCE COMPLETION

1. Someone will be needed to *proctor* the _____

   _____

2. The entire department *deplores* what _____

   _____

3. You had better *immerse* yourself in _____

   _____

---

a (f*a*t); ay (f*a*te); ah (f*a*r); au (d*ou*bt); ch (*ch*ur*ch*); e (s*e*lf, c*a*re); ee (*e*v*e*ning); ə (*a*bout); f (*f*lag, *ph*one); hw (*wh*ile); i (f*i*t); iy (k*i*te); ŋ (li*nk*, si*ng*); o (*au*dio, c*o*rn); ow (*o*pen); oo (c*oo*k); oi (*oi*l); sh (*sh*oe, ambi*ti*on); th (*th*ink); u (*u*p, l*o*ve); uw (*oo*ze); yu (c*u*re); yuw (*you*th, *u*nited); zh (plea*s*ure)

223

4. Can we ever really *fathom* the myths of _____

_____

5. The president has *proscribed* all those who _____

_____

6. Lady Norris will not *condescend* to _____

_____

7. You can *pique* Glendon with a single allusion to _____

_____

8. Did the mayor *intimate* any changes in _____

_____

9. Raymond says he has the facts to *impugn* the dean's _____

_____

10. Such a philosophical egalitarian naturally *espouses* _____

_____

11. Try to *distill* these ideas into _____

_____

12. Let's *devise* a new plan to _____

_____

13. These questions are intended to *elicit* _____

_____

14. Don't *chide* poor John for _____

_____

15. You may *incur* the instructor's displeasure simply by _____

_____

CRISSCROSS PUZZLE

ACROSS

1. To supervise or monitor
2. To suggest or make known indirectly
3. To scold in a mild manner
4. To denounce, banish, or condemn
5. To advocate, as a cause or movement
6. To plunge deeply into
7. To regret very strongly

DOWN

1. To concentrate, purify, or refine
2. To call into question by means of logical argument
3. To reduce oneself to a lower level; to patronize those of lower rank
4. To offend the pride of
5. To (try to) get to the bottom of
6. To draw out or cause to happen
7. To bring upon oneself
8. To think up or contrive

225

Action Words (2)

WORD LIST

1. abridge (ə-BRIJ): to shorten or condense
2. adduce (ə-DUWS): to bring forth as evidence
3. adulterate (ə-DUL-tə-*rayt*): to make impure or inferior
4. allure (ə-LOOR): to attract by trickery
5. assert (ə-SURT): to state in a positive manner
6. augment (og-MENT): to make (appear) greater
7. chortle (CHOR-təl): to speak and chuckle simultaneously
8. decipher (di-SIY-fər): to decode, as a message
9. decry (di-KRIY): to denounce openly and strongly
10. deem (DEEM): to judge, regard, or think
11. defer (di-FUR): to postpone or yield
12. demean (di-MEEN): to humble or sully, as one's character
13. disseminate (di-SEM-ə-*nayt*): to spread abroad
14. efface (i-FAYS): to wipe out or obliterate
15. ululate (YUWL-yə-*layt*): to howl, wail, or lament

SENTENCE COMPLETION

1. The committee *deemed* it necessary that _____

_____

2. If we *disseminate* this information soon enough, _____

_____

---

a (*fat*); ay (*fate*); ah (*far*); au (*do*ubt); ch (*church*); e (*self, care*); ee (*evening*); ə (*about*); f (*f*lag, *ph*one); hw (*wh*ile); i (*fit*); iy (*kite*); ŋ (*link, sing*); o (*audio, corn*); ow (*open*); oo (*cook*); oi (*oil*); sh (*sh*oe, ambi*ti*on); th (*th*ink); u (*up, love*); uw (*ooze*); yu (*cure*); yuw (*youth, united*); zh (plea*s*ure)

3. To *abridge* the facts in such a way is really to _____

_____

4. This fawning fellow always *defers* to _____

_____

5. Even domesticated dogs sometimes *ululate* the _____

_____

6. *Chortle* while you can, for _____

_____

7. These evildoers will try to *allure* you with _____

_____

8. I can't understand why anyone would *efface* _____

_____

9. As a free and independent people, we should *decry* the _____

_____

10. You will only *adulterate* what was a good product by _____

_____

11. By such statements, you *demean* all who _____

_____

12. When you *adduce* such damning evidence, you _____

_____

13. Do not *augment* this imposter's position by _____

_____

14. The accused adamantly *asserts* that _____

_____

15. No one can *decipher* this strange _____

_____

CRISSCROSS PUZZLE

ACROSS

1. To bring forth as evidence
2. To howl, wail, or lament
3. To shorten or condense
4. To decode, as a message
5. To state in a positive manner
6. To postpone or yield
7. To judge, regard, or think
8. To make (appear) greater

DOWN

1. To attract by trickery
2. To denounce openly and strongly
3. To humble or sully, as one's character
4. To wipe out or obliterate
5. To make impure or inferior
6. To spread abroad
7. To speak and chuckle simultaneously

Action Words (3)

WORD LIST

1. commiserate (kə-MIZ-ə-*rayt*): to feel honest pity for
2. comply (kəm-PLIY): to act in accordance with rules
3. comprise (kəm-PRIYZ): to make up or compose
4. denigrate (DEN-ə-*grayt*): to tarnish the reputation of
5. emulate (EM-yə-*layt*): to (try to) equal or surpass
6. encumber (in-KUM-bər): to load down
7. extol (ik-STOWL): to praise extravagantly
8. fructify (FRUK-tə-*fiy*): to make fruitful
9. fulminate (FUL-mə-*nayt*): to explode with violent denunciations
10. indemnify (in-DEM-nə-*fiy*): to protect against financial loss
11. lampoon (lam-PUWN): to ridicule in written satire
12. mutilate (MYUWT-əl-*ayt*): to damage or disfigure beyond repair
13. postulate (PAHS-chə-*layt*): to assume truth without proof
14. purport (pər-PORT): to claim or repute, often falsely
15. recant (ri-KANT): to formally renounce former statements

SENTENCE COMPLETION

1. All attempts to *denigrate* the character of _____

   _____

2. Only infrequently do we *extol* the _____

   _____

3. The press will surely *lampoon* the governor for _____

   _____

---

a (*fat*); ay (*fate*); ah (*far*); au (*doubt*); ch (*church*); e (*self, care*); ee (*evening*); ə (*about*); f (*flag, phone*); hw (*while*); i (*fit*); iy (*kite*); ŋ (*link, sing*); o (*audio, corn*); ow (*open*); oo (*cook*); oi (*oil*); sh (*shoe, ambition*); th (*think*); u (*up, love*); uw (*ooze*); yu (*cure*); yuw (*youth, united*); zh (*pleasure*)

4. Let's hire an advertising agency to *vivify* our _____

5. These new units can *oscillate* samples at _____

6. Circumstances dictate that the department *reduplicate* its _____

7. Hopefully, time will *ameliorate* the _____

8. Nothing can *exonerate* the criminal because _____

9. Reading will never be *supplanted* by _____

10. Inclement weather forced the marshal to *foreshorten* the _____

11. A night's rest should *replenish* _____

12. Why must you always *badger* those who _____

13. Please let me *dissuade* you from _____

14. I would be the last to *avow* that _____

15. The press shouldn't *depict* the president as _____

CRISSCROSS PUZZLE

ACROSS

1. To provide money for expenses
2. To make full or complete again
3. To obtain or secure, as for someone else
4. To persuade against
5. To make or become better
6. To swing back and forth, as between two points
7. To represent in words, pictures, sculpture, and the like

DOWN

1. To make more lively or animated
2. To take the place of something else
3. To double or repeat
4. To declare frankly and openly
5. To torment or harass
6. To present in an abridged form
7. To accuse of a crime
8. To prove guiltless

Action Words (8)

WORD LIST

1. belie (bi-LIY): to picture falsely or misrepresent
2. carouse (kə-RAUZ): to drink and have a good time
3. concur (kən-KUR): to agree with
4. deduce (di-DUWS): to conclude logically from a known premise
5. demur (di-MUR): to hesitate because of uncertainty
6. exhume (ig-ZYUWM): to bring to light (life) again
7. founder (FAUN-dər): to sink; to fail or collapse
8. immolate (IM-ə-*layt*): to kill as a sacrifice
9. oust (AUST): to force out, as from a position
10. polarize (POW-lə-*riyz*): to break up into opposing groups
11. propagate (PRAHP-ə-*gayt*): to reproduce in great numbers
12. reproach (ri-PROWCH): to shame or disgrace
13. retrench (ri-TRENCH): to economize (systematically)
14. rhapsodize (RAP-sə-*diyz*): to talk (sing) with extravagant feeling
15. spawn (SPON): to produce many offspring

SENTENCE COMPLETION

1. The tribal chief offered to *immolate* his own daughter to _____

   _____

2. Don't let your career *founder* on _____

   _____

3. The national committee will soon *oust* these _____

   _____

---

a (fat);   ay (fate);   ah (far);   au (doubt);   ch (church);   e (self, care);   ee (evening);   ə (about);   f (flag, phone);   hw (while);   i (fit);   iy (kite);   ŋ (link, sing);   o (audio, corn);   ow (open);   oo (cook);   oi (oil);   sh (shoe, ambition);   th (think);   u (up, love);   uw (ooze);   yu (cure);   yuw (youth, united);   zh (pleasure)

4. Every type of disease can *propagate* in _____

_____

5. The accounting department says that we must *retrench* all _____

_____

6. Spring is traditionally the season to *rhapsodize* about _____

_____

7. The speaker *reproached* his audience with _____

_____

8. Such dedicated terrorists are likely to *spawn* _____

_____

9. It was the proposed amendment that really *polarized* the _____

_____

10. I can *deduce* little or nothing from what _____

_____

11. Not even your strongest supporters will *concur* with you on _____

_____

12. The time may soon come when we *exhume* some _____

_____

13. Clearly, your loud boasting *belies* your _____

_____

14. Let's *carouse* for a day or two and then _____

_____

15. Do not *demur* when the king _____

_____

CRISSCROSS PUZZLE

ACROSS

1. To bring to light (life) again
2. To drink and have a good time
3. To economize (systematically)
4. To hesitate because of uncertainty
5. To reproduce in great numbers
6. To sink; to fail or collapse
7. To force out, as from a position
8. To agree with

DOWN

1. To produce many offspring
2. To picture falsely or misrepresent
3. To talk (sing) with extravagant feeling
4. To conclude logically from a known premise
5. To shame or disgrace
6. To kill as a sacrifice
7. To break up into opposing groups

Action Words (9)

WORD LIST

1. adorn (ə-DORN):   to ornament with anything nice
2. blandish (BLAN-dish):   to coax by the use of flattery
3. correlate (KOR-ə-*layt*):   to bring into a mutual relationship
4. defile (di-FIYL):   to make unclean or impure
5. denude (di-NUWD):   to lay waste or strip bare
6. devastate (DEV-ə-*stayt*):   to destroy altogether
7. expurgate (EKS-pər-*gayt*):   to remove all objectionable passages from
8. extrapolate (ik-STRAP-ə-*layt*):   to speculate on the unknown or make judgments on the unknown from the known
9. fabricate (FAB-rə-*kayt*):   to make up or assemble
10. festoon (fes-TUWN):   to decorate elaborately, as with garlands
11. inveigle (in-VEE-gəl):   to deceive by clever enticement
12. precipitate (pri-SIP-ə-*tayt*):   to cause to happen at once
13. regress (ri-GRES):   to go backward
14. repudiate (ri-PYUW-dee-*ayt*):   to disown or deny any relationship with
15. shuttle (SHUT-əl):   to move (travel) back and forth frequently

SENTENCE COMPLETION

1. If you *regress* much more, you will _____

    _____

2. The corporation president *shuttles* between _____

    _____

3. These letters may *precipitate* another _____

    _____

---

a (*fat*);   ay (*fate*);   ah (*far*);   au (*doubt*);   ch (*church*);   e (*self, care*);   ee (*evening*);   ə (*about*);   f (*flag, phone*);   hw (*while*);   i (*fit*);   iy (*kite*);   ŋ (*link, sing*);   o (*audio, corn*);   ow (*open*);   oo (*cook*);   oi (*oil*);   sh (*shoe, ambition*);   th (*think*);   u (*up, love*);   uw (*ooze*);   yu (*cure*);   yuw (*youth, united*);   zh (*pleasure*)

4. We can *extrapolate* little from _____

_____

5. Dame Edith often *adorns* herself with _____

_____

6. Curtis tried to *repudiate* his entire _____

_____

7. That credulous character was *inveigled* into _____

_____

8. The approaching waters are certain to *devastate* the _____

_____

9. Perhaps the two divisions could *correlate* their _____

_____

10. If you *blandish* him cleverly enough, he _____

_____

11. Christmas is the season to *festoon* the _____

_____

12. Why should we *expurgate* the novel just to _____

_____

13. This particular compound can *denude* a _____

_____

14. Perhaps we can *fabricate* some story which _____

_____

15. These people *defile* the sanctuary simply by _____

_____

CRISSCROSS PUZZLE

ACROSS

1. To make unclean or impure
2. To make up or assemble
3. To cause to happen at once
4. To move (travel) back and forth frequently
5. To speculate on the unknown or make judgments on the unknown from the known
6. To ornament with anything nice
7. To destroy altogether
8. To go backward

DOWN

1. To decorate elaborately, as with garlands
2. To coax by the use of flattery
3. To bring into a mutual relationship
4. To remove all objectionable passages from
5. To lay waste or strip bare
6. To deceive by clever enticement
7. To disown or deny any relationship with

Action Words (10)

1. abscond (ab-SKAHND): to run away and hide
2. blaspheme (blas-FEEM): to curse or slander
3. codify (KAHD-ə-*fiy*): to arrange in a systematic collection
4. consummate (KAHN-sə-*mayt*): to bring to fulfillment
5. cordon (KOR-dən): to encircle or blockade
6. deride (di-RIYD): to make fun of or ridicule
7. disconcert (*dis*-kən-SURT): to embarrass or confuse
8. evoke (i-VOWK): to call up or bring forth
9. expend (ik-SPEND): to use up or exhaust
10. exploit (ek-SPLOIT): to take unfair advantage of for profit
11. extricate (EK-strə-*kayt*): to free from entanglements
12. flout (FLAUT): to scoff at, scorn, or mock
13. importune (*im*-por-TUWN): to annoy with persistent requests
14. incarcerate (in-KAHR-sə-*rayt*): to shut up or imprison
15. mesmerize (MEZ-mə-*riyz*): to hold hypnotically; to fascinate

SENTENCE COMPLETION

1. You may *evoke* the powers of all the gods, but you _____

_____

2. Dennis *flouts* authority as if _____

_____

3. The dancers *mesmerized* Heathcliff as he _____

_____

---

a (f*a*t);   ay (f*a*te);   ah (f*a*r);   au (d*ou*bt);   ch (*ch*ur*ch*);   e (s*e*lf, c*a*re);   ee (*e*vening);   ə (*a*bout);   f (*f*lag, *ph*one);   hw (*wh*ile);   i (f*i*t);   iy (k*i*te);   ŋ (li*n*k, si*ng*);   o (*au*dio, c*o*rn);   ow (*o*pen);   oo (c*oo*k);   oi (*oi*l);   sh (*sh*oe, ambi*ti*on);   th (*th*ink);   u (*u*p, l*o*ve);   uw (*oo*ze);   yu (c*u*re);   yuw (*you*th, *u*nited);   zh (plea*s*ure)

4. Do we really *exploit* countries that _____

_____

5. I must again *importune* you to _____

_____

6. Relax; don't *expend* so much _____

_____

7. It is impious to *blaspheme* against _____

_____

8. Years will be needed to *codify* all the _____

_____

9. *Cordon* off the area and then _____

_____

10. Arnold's presence will *disconcert* all those _____

_____

11. Only a fool would *abscond* with _____

_____

12. Nature has *incarcerated* all of us in _____

_____

13. Lawrence is being unfairly *derided* for his _____

_____

14. The trustees want to *consummate* the agreement so _____

_____

15. Sidney has been unable to *extricate* himself from _____

_____

CRISSCROSS PUZZLE

ACROSS

1. To take unfair advantage of for profit
2. To make fun of or ridicule
3. To hold hypnotically; to fascinate
4. To arrange in a systematic collection
5. To bring to fulfillment
6. To scoff at, scorn, or mock
7. To shut up or imprison

DOWN

1. To use up or exhaust
2. To encircle or blockade
3. To embarrass or confuse
4. To run away and hide
5. To curse or slander
6. To free from entanglements
7. To call up or bring forth
8. To annoy with persistent requests

Chapter 6

Descriptive Words

From the final chapter of Part One, "Words with Suffixes," you are already familiar with descriptive words. In the sentence fill-in exercises of that chapter, you indicated the parts of speech—adjectives, nouns, or verbs—of the words as they were used in the sentences. This chapter, then, builds on that one, concentrating on adjectives.

A good store of descriptive words—adjectives—is indispensable for anyone who hopes to use language with precision. Descriptive words are for the writer what fine tints and delicate hues are for the painter. Notice how the following rather vague sentences are improved by the use of an appropriate and precise adjective:

> *vague:* Tim likes to be around a lot of people.
> *improved:* Tim is a *gregarious* individual.

> *vague:* Edgar ate his dinner as if he were very hungry.
> *improved:* Edgar ate his dinner with *ravenous* intensity.

> *vague:* The weather was too bad for us to enjoy the outing.
> *improved:* *Inclement* weather ruined the outing.

> *vague:* Calling me delicate is the same thing as saying I am a weakling.
> *improved:* Calling me delicate is *tantamount* to saying I am a weakling.

> *vague:* I will never be able to forget the impression Mr. Hobbins made on my life.
> *improved:* Mr. Hobbins made an *indelible* impression on my life.

253

vague:	The forest is pretty and unspoiled.
improved:	The forest has a *pristine* beauty.
vague:	People who always sit around doing nothing are seldom interested in physical activity.
improved:	*Sedentary* people are seldom interested in physical activity.
vague:	The sunset was very colorful.
improved:	The *kaleidoscopic* colors of the sunset were brilliant.

The relationship between verbs and adjectives is closer than you might expect. By simply adding *-ing* or *-ed* to many verbs, you can form a word that functions as a precise and forceful adjective. Of course, you have to place the word in a sentence to appreciate what a good descriptive word it has become. As you look at the following examples, note that some verbs drop an *e* before adding *-ing,* and others require only the addition of *-d* rather than *-ed*:

verb

abridge	The *abridged* edition of the novel was two hundred pages shorter than the original.
demean	What a *demeaning* experience the examination was.
denigrate	Such *denigrating* statements are not intended to flatter.
mutilate	The *mutilated* body of the victim was found in an abandoned mining camp.
scintillate	What a *scintillating* tale the old fellow told us.
bluster	The *blustering* fool would listen to no one.
acclaim	Though a highly *acclaimed* expert in the field, Dr. Thomas admitted that he didn't know what to make of the discovery.
enervate	An *enervating* drug was used to subdue the excited researcher.

The odd-numbered and even-numbered sequences in this chapter differ from each other, although the patterns are the same within each odd-numbered and each even-numbered sequence. After the initial word list, the odd-numbered sequences contain a regular sentence fill-in exercise and a "Definition and Antonym Matching" exercise in which you match both a definition and an antonym with each vocabulary word. *Antonyms* are words with opposite meanings, and the lists of antonyms immediately follow the lists of definitions. This exercise is in turn followed by a review sentence fill-in. In this final exercise you are given a list of six verbs from Part One of the book. These verbs are to be converted into *-ed* or *-ing* adjectives and inserted into the sentences below the list.

The even-numbered sequences include a crisscross puzzle following the initial word list. Each puzzle contains eighteen descriptive words, always drawn from the preceding odd-numbered sequence and the even-numbered sequence on which you are working. Thus, the crisscross in the second sequence contains words from both the first and second sequences; the crisscross in the fourth sequence contains words from both the third and fourth sequences. The specific words which fit into the puzzles are listed just below each puzzle. The final exercises in the sequence are a pair of six-word, six-sentence matching exercises. The sentences in these two exercises contain short definitions [in brackets] rather than blanks, and you are to match the appropriate words with the sentences.

Descriptive Words (1)

WORD LIST

1. abrasive (ə-BRAY-siv):   irritating in a harsh, grinding manner
2. bizarre (bi-ZAHR):   odd or unexpected, as in manner or appearance
3. complaisant (kəm-PLAY-zənt):   inclined always to be pleasant; obliging
4. concave (kahn-KAYV):   curved inward like the hollow of a ball
5. convex (kahn-VEKS):   curved or bulged outward
6. flamboyant (flam-BOI-ənt):   extravagantly showy; elaborate
7. frugal (FRUW-gəl):   very sparing and close with money; scanty
8. prolific (prow-LIF-ik):   producing great numbers of anything
9. rancid (RAN-sid):   smelling or tasting rotten; foul
10. sinister (SIN-is-tər):   seeming to promise evil or misfortune
11. ubiquitous (yuw-BIK-wə-təs):   seeming to be everywhere at once; in the way
12. verdant (VUR-dənt):   green (growing) with fresh vegetation

SENTENCE FILL-IN

1. Centuries of winter floods have worn a series of _____ indentations along the stone walls of the creek bed.

2. I run into this _____ character everywhere I go.

3. The _____ Highlands of Scotland are marvelous in the springtime.

4. When your subordinates become too _____ to point out your blunders, it is time to replace them.

5. A most _____ writer, Hotchkiss produces two novels every year.

6. The most _____ sound I have ever heard is a lion purring.

7. Though the film had a strange and _____ plot, the characters were believable enough.

a (fat);   ay (fate);   ah (far);   au (doubt);   ch (church);   e (self, care);   ee (evening);   ə (about);   f (flag, phone);   hw (while);   i (fit);   iy (kite);   ŋ (link, sing);   o (audio, corn);   ow (open);   oo (cook);   oi (oil);   sh (shoe, ambition);   th (think);   u (up, love);   uw (ooze);   yu (cure);   yuw (youth, united);   zh (pleasure)

255

8. A _____ dresser, Lucian thinks nothing of wearing a pink suit and alligator shoes.

9. The _____ smell of rotting flesh came from the tannery.

10. The perfectly _____ shape of the mound suggests that it may be part of the Indian burial grounds.

11. When such _____ remarks come from one you respect and admire, they are particularly displeasing.

12. The desert is indeed a _____ provider for its denizens.

DEFINITION AND ANTONYM MATCHING

DEF   ANT

_____ _____ 1. ubiquitous

_____ _____ 2. abrasive

_____ _____ 3. verdant

_____ _____ 4. bizarre

_____ _____ 5. sinister

_____ _____ 6. complaisant

_____ _____ 7. rancid

_____ _____ 8. concave

_____ _____ 9. prolific

_____ _____ 10. convex

_____ _____ 11. frugal

_____ _____ 12. flamboyant

DEFINITIONS

a. curved or bulged outward
b. inclined always to be pleasant; obliging
c. seeming to promise evil or misfortune
d. seeming to be everywhere at once; in the way
e. irritating in a harsh, grinding manner
f. extravagantly showy; elaborate
g. very sparing and close with money; scanty
h. odd or unexpected, as in manner or appearance
i. smelling or tasting rotten; foul
j. green (growing) with fresh vegetation
k. producing great numbers of anything
l. curved inward like the hollow of a ball

ANTONYMS

a. conservative
b. optimistic
c. wasteful
d. commonplace
e. absent
f. convex
g. sterile
h. soothing
i. parched
j. concave
k. antagonistic
l. fresh

REVIEW SENTENCE FILL-IN

Write the adjective form (-*ing* or -*ed*) of the following verbs from Part One in the blanks of the appropriate sentences below.

allocate   homogenize   intervene
galvanize   ingratiate   reclaim

1. The young candidate's _____ smile irritated many of the people in the audience.

2. In a politically _____ society there is little or no room for dissent.

3. All _____ funds must be spent by the end of the fiscal year.

4. In the _____ years, many of my old classmates became fat and lazy.

5. _____ steel is covered with a zinc plate.

6. All the _____ land is now mysteriously contaminated by some deadly chemical.

Descriptive Words (2)

WORD LIST

1. emotive (i-MOW-tiv): related to the emotions
2. fetid (FET-id): having a rotten smell
3. idyllic (iy-DIL-ik): romantically picturesque
4. nebulous (NEB-yə-ləs): vague and indistinct
5. opulent (AHP-yə-lənt): showing wealth and abundance
6. pastoral (PAS-tər-əl): characteristic of an idealized view of rural life
7. peremptory (pə-REMP-tə-ree): decisive and dictatorial
8. precipitous (pri-SIP-ə-təs): steep, sheer; instantaneous
9. raucous (RO-kəs): loud and rowdy
10. serpentine (SUR-pən-*teen*): winding in and out
11. tepid (TEP-id): just slightly warm
12. viable (VIY-ə-bəl): able to sustain life

CRISSCROSS PUZZLE

ACROSS

1. Producing great numbers of anything
2. Inclined always to be pleasant; obliging
3. Able to sustain life
4. Romantically picturesque
5. Related to the emotions
6. Seeming to be everywhere at once; in the way
7. Decisive and dictatorial
8. Characteristic of an idealized view of rural life
9. Curved inward like the hollow of a ball

DOWN

1. Vague and indistinct
2. Winding in and out
3. Steep, sheer; instantaneous
4. Extravagantly showy; elaborate
5. Seeming to promise evil or misfortune
6. Just slightly warm
7. Irritating in a harsh, grinding manner
8. Green (growing) with fresh vegetation
9. Having a rotten smell

---

a (*a*t); ay (*fa*te); ah (*fa*r); au (*dou*bt); ch (*church*); e (s*e*lf, c*a*re); ee (*e*vening); ə (*a*bout); f (*f*lag, *ph*one); hw (*wh*ile); i (*fi*t); iy (*ki*te); ŋ (li*n*k, si*ng*); o (*au*dio, *co*rn); ow (*o*pen); oo (*coo*k); oi (*oi*l); sh (*sh*oe, ambi*ti*on); th (*th*ink); u (*u*p, l*o*ve); uw (*ooze*); yu (*cu*re); yuw (*you*th, *u*nited); zh (plea*s*ure)

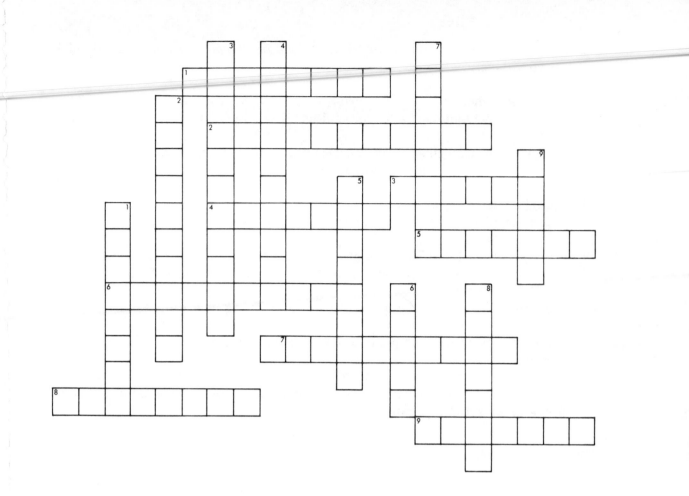

Words included in the puzzle are *abrasive, complaisant, concave, emotive, fetid, flamboyant, idyllic, nebulous, pastoral, peremptory, precipitous, prolific, serpentine, sinister, tepid, ubiquitous, verdant,* and *viable.*

SENTENCE MATCHING

a. fetid   c. opulent   e. serpentine
b. idyllic   d. peremptory   f. viable

_____ 1. Such an [*showing wealth and abundance*] display of jewels in public is dangerous with so many thieves around.

_____ 2. A space station should not be considered totally [*able to sustain life*] until it can produce its own food.

_____ 3. The wound became [*having a rotten smell*] after only an hour's neglect.

_____ 4. A narrow, [*winding in and out*] pathway led us through the wilderness to the tiny settlement.

_____ 5. So [*decisive and dictatorial*] an attitude allows little room for questions or criticism.

_____ 6. Once again the poet has painted an [*romantically picturesque*] portrait of his native village.

        g. emotive   i. pastoral   k. raucous

        h. nebulous   j. precipitous   l. tepid

_____ 7. Any president who gives away American territory is likely to experience a [*steep, sheer; instantaneous*] decline in popularity.

_____ 8. Though [*related to the emotions*] approaches to teaching have been popular for several years now, there is little evidence of their superiority over other methods.

_____ 9. We were amazed that so pleasant a [*characteristic of an idealized view of rural life*] scene could exist so close to a metropolitan area the size of London.

_____10. A [*just slightly warm*] cup of tea is as disappointing as a limp handshake.

_____11. If, indeed, you made your point, it was so [*vague and indistinct*] that few people noticed.

_____12. Though the party may have become a little [*loud and rowdy*] after midnight, things never got out of hand.

Descriptive Words (3)

WORD LIST

1. brackish (BRAK-ish):   having an unpleasant (somewhat salty) taste
2. callow (KAL-ow):   literally, still without enough feathers to fly; immature
3. debonair (deb-ə-NER):   easily cheerful and friendly
4. diffusive (di-FYUW-siv):   tending to spread out in all directions
5. ersatz (UR-zahts):   typical of a substitute of inferior quality
6. germane (jər-MAYN):   specifically related to the point
7. impervious (im-PUR-vee-əs):   incapable of being penetrated
8. malleable (MAL-ee-ə-bəl):   capable of being reshaped; flexuous
9. proletarian (prow-lə-TER-ee-ən):   related to ordinary working people
10. strident (STRIYD-ənt):   painfully grating to the ears
11. sylvan (SIL-vən):   related (romantically) to the woods and forests
12. truculent (TRUK-yə-lənt):   rude in a fierce, cruel, and warlike manner

SENTENCE FILL-IN

1. These savages are a _____ people, ready to fight at the slightest provocation.

2. Though he was once a _____ young fellow, Thayer is now a hardnosed executive.

3. The little college is located in an unspoiled _____ valley in Vermont.

4. The _____ dramatics of television soap operas bear little resemblance to real life.

5. Isn't it amazing how much more _____ we become after we learn that the world wasn't created the day before we were born?

6. America has made a virtue of establishing a _____ society without preaching collectivism.

---

a (fat);   ay (fate);   ah (far);   au (doubt);   ch (church);   e (self, care);   ee (evening);   ə (about);   f (flag, phone);   hw (while);   i (fit);   iy (kite);   ŋ (link, sing);   o (audio, corn);   ow (open);   oo (cook);   oi (oil);   sh (shoe, ambition);   th (think);   u (up, love);   uw (ooze);   yu (cure);   yuw (youth, united);   zh (pleasure)

7. It is difficult to reason with people whose minds are _____ to logical thought.

8. Such _____ opinions suggest an individual of little experience.

9. The well water at camp tasted harsh and _____.

10. If Mother's voice was sometimes _____, her heart was nonetheless malleable.

11. These facts are interesting, but they are not _____ to the case we are considering.

12. The article said that the feminist movement has become so _____ that it no longer has unified political clout.

DEFINITION AND ANTONYM MATCHING

DEF   ANT

_____ _____ 1. ersatz

_____ _____ 2. sylvan

_____ _____ 3. brackish

_____ _____ 4. germane

_____ _____ 5. proletarian

_____ _____ 6. strident

_____ _____ 7. callow

_____ _____ 8. malleable

_____ _____ 9. diffusive

_____ _____ 10. truculent

_____ _____ 11. debonair

_____ _____ 12. impervious

DEFINITIONS

a. having an unpleasant (somewhat salty) taste
b. capable of being reshaped; flexuous
c. painfully grating to the ears
d. literally, still without enough feathers to fly; immature
e. typical of a substitute of inferior quality
f. related (romantically) to the woods and forests
g. specifically related to the point
h. related to ordinary working people
i. easily cheerful and friendly
j. incapable of being penetrated
k. rude in a fierce, cruel, and warlike manner
l. tending to spread out in all directions

ANTONYMS

a. aristocratic
b. bona fide
c. peaceable
e. converging
e. melodic
f. receptive
g. morose
h. bland
i. urban
j. rigid
k. irrelevant
l. adult

Descriptive Words (5)

WORD LIST

1. aromatic (*ar*-ə-MAT-ik): fragrant, spicy, or sweet smelling
2. cogent (KOW-jənt): to the point in a forceful and compelling way
3. facetious (fə-SEE-shəs): (inappropriately) jocular or ironic; humorous
4. gauche (GOWSH): with little or no social grace
5. indigenous (in-DIJ-ə-nəs): native to a particular region
6. intransigent (in-TRAN-sə-jənt): incapable of compromising
7. macabre (mə-KAHB-rə): horrible and strange, as with grim detail
8. maudlin (MOD-lin): (drunkenly) sentimental
9. opaque (ow-PAYK): not allowing light to pass through; dark
10. paramount (PAR-ə-*maunt*): of supreme rank or importance
11. spurious (SPYUR-ee-əs): without authenticity or validity; counterfeit
12. turgid (TUR-jid): swollen or pompous, as with conceit; distended

SENTENCE FILL-IN

1. A college degree, not a marriage certificate, remains Ruth's _____ concern.

2. Upon closer examination, what had seemed like a good proposal proved to be

   _____ .

3. The office manager's apparent addiction to _____ remarks usually gets him the glib response he deserves.

4. Although your arguments in favor of the proposal are quite _____ , the decision has already been made to reject it.

5. Since both labor and management remained _____ , the strike continued through the Christmas holidays.

6. That pipe tobacco may smell _____ to you, but it is about to run me out of the room.

---

a (fat); ay (fate); ah (far); au (doubt); ch (church); e (self, care); ee (evening); ə (about); f (flag, phone); hw (while); i (fit); iy (kite); ŋ (link, sing); o (audio, corn); ow (open); oo (cook); oi (oil); sh (shoe, ambition); th (think); u (up, love); uw (ooze); yu (cure); yuw (youth, united); zh (pleasure)

9. The ravenous soldiers stared in disbelief at the _____ turkey in the center of the table.

10. Tom's _____ remark cut his father to the heart.

11. Though the wounded soldier is still alive, he holds on by the most _____ of threads.

12. With the great diversity of clothing being worn these days, it is difficult to know what

    is _____ and what is not.

DEFINITION AND ANTONYM MATCHING

DEF   ANT

DEFINITIONS

_____ _____ 1. egalitarian

_____ _____ 2. modish

_____ _____ 3. adamant

_____ _____ 4. trenchant

_____ _____ 5. ethereal

_____ _____ 6. sinuous

_____ _____ 7. tenuous

_____ _____ 8. chivalrous

_____ _____ 9. inclement

_____ _____ 10. succulent

_____ _____ 11. insouciant

_____ _____ 12. capricious

a. rich, juicy, or full of interest
b. showing no mercy or leniency; harsh
c. likely to change without reason or warning
d. in the most current fashion
e. related to a belief in human equality
f. forceful in a keen and penetrating manner
g. generally carefree and unbothered
h. as hard as (metal) stone; unyielding
i. of a more delicate quality than ordinary things
j. slender, fine, or flimsy
k. possessing the noble qualities of a knight
l. winding in and out; crooked

ANTONYMS

a. tasteless
b. autocratic
c. uptight
d. indecisive
e. relenting
f. impolite
g. common
h. linear
i. stocky
j. obsolete
k. benign
l. steadfast

REVIEW SENTENCE FILL-IN

Write the adjective form (*-ing* or *-ed*) of the following verbs from Part One in the blanks of the appropriate sentences below.

confound enlighten modulate
vilify   interrogate revitalize

1. The meeting was most _____; now we know the problems that we face.

2. A _____ central city is the goal of the urban council.

3. Our top secret agent has sent a message so _____ that the entire agency is in a state of confusion.

4. A carefully _____ tone came from each of the speakers.

5. The instructor's _____ manner made me feel as if I were on trial.

6. These _____ stories about the candidate's private life will ruin his chances for election.

Descriptive Words (8)

WORD LIST

1. circuitous (sər-KYUW-ə-təs): roundabout or devious
2. derisive (di-RIY-siv): ridiculing or scornful
3. dulcet (DUL-sit): soothing and melodious
4. motley (MAHT-lee): many-colored or assorted
5. ominous (AHM-ə-nəs): threatening subsequent misfortune or disaster
6. onerous (AHN-ər-əs): laborious in a drawn-out, tedious sense
7. passé (pa-SAY): old-fashioned and out of date
8. ponderous (PAHN-dər-əs): of so great a weight as to be dull and defeating
9. rabid (RAB-id): fanatically devoted
10. resurgent (ri-SUR-jənt): coming to life again
11. saturnine (SAT-ər-*niyn*): disposed, as if by birth, to be gloomy
12. tawny (TO-nee): a yellowish brown

CRISSCROSS PUZZLE

ACROSS

1. Related to a belief in human equality
2. Likely to change without reason or warning
3. Of a more delicate quality than ordinary things
4. Generally carefree and unbothered
5. Old-fashioned and out of date
6. Slender, fine, or flimsy
7. Many-colored or assorted
8. Showing no mercy or leniency
9. Fanatically devoted

DOWN

1. Of so great a weight as to be dull and defeating
2. In the most current fashion
3. Laborious in a drawn-out, tedious sense
4. Rich, juicy, or full of interest
5. As hard as (metal) stone
6. Roundabout or devious
7. Soothing and melodious
8. Disposed, as if by birth, to be gloomy
9. Threatening subsequent misfortune or disaster

---

a (fat); ay (fate); ah (far); au (doubt); ch (church); e (self, care); ee (evening); ə (about); f (flag, phone); hw (while); i (fit); iy (kite); ŋ (link, sing); o (audio, corn); ow (open); oo (cook); oi (oil); sh (shoe, ambition); th (think); u (up, love); uw (ooze); yu (cure); yuw (youth, united); zh (pleasure)

Words included in this puzzle are *adamant, capricious, circuitous, dulcet, egalitarian, ethereal, inclement, insouciant, modish, motley, ominous, onerous, passé, ponderous, rabid, saturnine, succulent* and *tenuous.*

SENTENCE MATCHING

a. circuitous   c. onerous   e. saturnine
b. dulcet   d. passé   f. tawny

_____ 1. Feminists have at last convinced many men that the sometimes [*laborious in a drawn-out, tedious sense*] tasks of child rearing and housekeeping should be shared by husband and wife.

_____ 2. Please cease your [*roundabout or devious*] ramblings and come to the point.

_____ 3. The tribe of victorious warriors drank large steins of [*yellowish brown*] ale and sang songs of heroes long dead.

Descriptive Words (10)

WORD LIST

1. apian (AY-pee-ən): related to or like bees
2. droll (DROWL): ironically humorous or oddly amusing
3. incipient (in-SIP-ee-ənt): in the earliest stages; just beginning
4. irresolute (i-REZ-ə-*luwt*): wavering in holding to a decision
5. jejune (ji-JUWN): uninteresting, empty, or childish
6. kaleidoscopic (kə-*liy*-də-SKAHP-ik): displaying intricate color patterns
7. officious (ə-FISH-əs): too efficient and helpful
8. palpable (PAL-pə-bəl): easily capable of perception by the senses
9. quintessential (*kwin*-tə-SEN-shəl): of a pure or perfect example of anything
10. regal (REE-gəl): like royalty
11. salutary (SAL-yə-*ter*-ee): conducive to health and happiness
12. surreptitious (*sur*-əp-TISH-əs): performed in a secret, underhanded way

CRISSCROSS PUZZLE

ACROSS

1. Displaying intricate color patterns
2. Unnecessarily grisly or gruesome
3. Doubtful, hesitant, or uncertain
4. Present, but in a dormant state
5. Related to or like bees
6. Covered with hair; shaggy
7. Without ordinary (sexual) restraints or control
8. Uninteresting, empty, or childish
9. In the earliest stages; just beginning

DOWN

1. Performed in secret, usually for illicit purposes
2. Done according to proper procedure
3. Ill-mannered and hard to get along with
4. Of a pure or perfect example
5. Conducive to health and happiness
6. Like royalty
7. Equal to; the same thing as
8. Too efficient and helpful
9. Disposed to be uncommunicative

---

a (fat); ay (fate); ah (far); au (doubt); ch (church); e (self, care); ee (evening); ə (about); f (flag, phone); hw (while); i (fit); iy (kite); ŋ (link, sing); o (audio, corn); ow (open); oo (cook); oi (oil); sh (shoe, ambition); th (think); u (up, love); uw (ooze); yu (cure); yuw (youth, united); zh (pleasure)

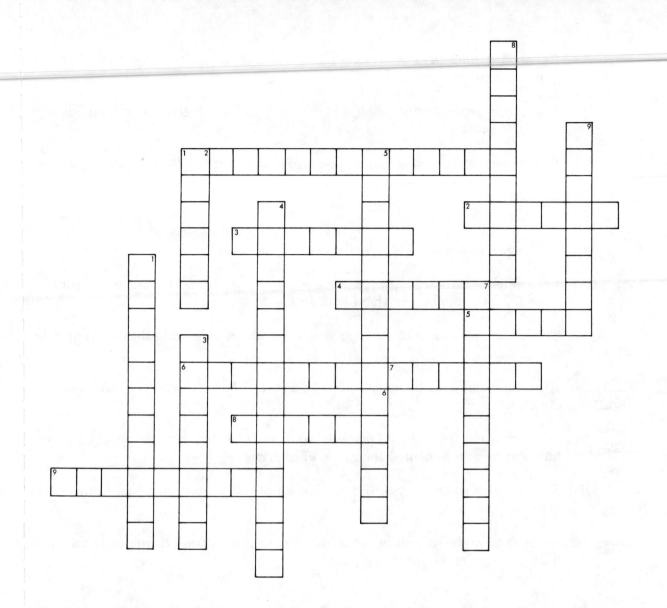

Words included in the puzzle are *apian, churlish, clandestine, dubious, hirsute, incipient, jejune, kaleidoscopic, kosher, latent, morbid, officious, quintessential, regal, salutary, taciturn, tantamount,* and *wanton.*

SENTENCE MATCHING

a. droll   c. kaleidoscopic   e. regal
b. incipient   d. palpable   f. surreptitous

_____ 1. A [*displaying intricate color patterns*] display of warm hues danced across the walls of the canyon as the sun passed through the billowy clouds.

_____ 2. When news of the [*performed in a secret, underhanded way*] meeting was leaked to the press, the conspirators knew they were in trouble.

_____ 3. I do not understand how the entire accounting department could have overlooked such a [*easily capable of perception by the senses*] error.

_____ 4. Norwood's [*ironically humorous or oddly amusing*] anecdotes make him a popular guest at campus parties.

_____ 5. The young prince's [*like royalty*] attire made him look like something out of a romantic novel.

_____ 6. I detect an [*in the earliest stages; just beginning*] hostility between the employees who have been with the company for some time and those who have been hired recently.

g. apian	i. jejune	k. quintessential
h. irresolute	j. officious	l. salutary

_____ 7. I see nothing artistically [*uninteresting, empty, or childish*] about many popular novels; I read numbers of them with interest.

_____ 8. The [*conducive to health and happiness*] effects of love and affection cannot be exaggerated.

_____ 9. A society dominated by legions of [*related to or like bees*] workers is not my idea of utopia.

_____10. "God save me from these [*too efficient and helpful*] fools who would run my business to ruin!" shouted the aging entrepreneur.

_____11. Four times now this [*wavering in holding to a decision*] man has changed his vote.

_____12. Here we have the [*of a pure or perfect example of anything*] clown; he is unhappy unless he can make people laugh.

Chapter 7

Words from Names

The study of the history and development of words is called *etymology*. You were involved to some extent in the study of etymology in Chapters 1 and 2, "Words from Latin Roots" and "Words from Greek Roots," when you learned new words by noting their relationship to Latin and Greek roots. Remember the words "animated," "inanimate," and "magnanimous"? Because all three contain the Latin root *anim*, meaning "life" or "spirit," we called them derivatives of the root *anim*. Such a consideration is a part of etymology.

Another aspect of etymology involves the people who have contributed their names to the formation of words in our language. The word "sandwich" provides a clear example of a person lending his name to the formation of a word. John Montagu, fourth earl of Sandwich, an eighteenth-century Englishman, was a man of questionable reputation. Not only was he incompetent and thoroughly corrupt as first lord of the Admiralty, but he was also openly immoral in his personal affairs. Gambling was one of his many vices, and during one twenty-four-hour marathon at the table, the earl is said to have refused to stop even to eat. Instead, he ordered that slices of bread, with thick slabs of roast beef stuffed between them, be brought to him so he could eat while playing. Thus, the notion of the sandwich, as well as the word, was born.

Similarly, we have the word "tawdry," meaning "cheap, ornate, or showy." In the sixth or seventh century, there was a pious Anglo-Saxon princess named Etheldreda. During her youth, Etheldreda loved expensive necklaces, especially pieces made of

5. All of our _____ measures notwithstanding, it appears that there will be no peace.

6. Though _____ may be the topic of locker-room jokes, it is a pathological condition that is hardly laughable.

7. Following our long day on the trail, the simple meal we prepared tasted like

_____.

8. You have been forewarned not to let the beauty's _____ manner tempt you.

9. Muhammad Ali's _____ antics in the ring diminished as he approached retirement.

10. The directions say that these drugs must be carefully stored in _____ containers.

MATCHING

_____ 1. terpsichorean

_____ 2. aeolian harp

_____ 3. nymphomania

_____ 4. ambrosia

_____ 5. mnemonics

_____ 6. Apollonian

_____ 7. jovial

_____ 8. Circean

_____ 9. irenic

_____ 10. hermetic

a. disciplined, serene, and well balanced
b. any technique or formula for aiding the memory
c. airtight; obscure; hard to understand
d. a stringed, boxlike instrument that produces music from the wind
e. anything that tastes (smells) good enough to be eaten by the gods
f. related (humorously) to dancing
g. uncontrollable sexual desire in a woman
h. filled with hearty good humor; genial
i. like a woman who can destroy men with her fascination and charm
j. tending to promote peace; pacific

Words from Names in Mythology (4)

WORD LIST

1. Amazonian (*am*-ə-ZOW-nee-ən): from the Amazons, a tribe of female warriors who lived in Scythia: characteristic of a large, powerful, aggressive woman

2. Antaean (an-TEE-ən): from Antaeus, a giant wrestler who was invincible as long as he was touching the earth: almost invincible; possessing superhuman strength

3. Argus-eyed (AHR-gəs-*iyd*): from Argus, a hundred-eyed giant ordered to guard Princess Io: always awake, vigilant, and observant

4. calliope (kə-LIY-ə-pee): from Calliope, mother of Orpheus and Muse of heroic poetry: a keyboard musical instrument with a series of steam whistles

5. erotica (i-RAHT-i-kə): from Eros, the Greek god of love: art and literature treating the subject of sexual love

6. heroine (HER-ə-win): from Hero, a priestess of Aphrodite who met her lover Leander nightly until he drowned coming to her: the major female character in a novel or play

7. Icarian (i-KER-ee-ən): from Icarus, who was drowned in the sea when he flew too close to the sun and melted his wax wings: foolishly daring

8. morphine (MOR-feen): from Morpheus, the Greek god of dreams: a drug that reduces pain and induces sleep

9. saturnalia (*sat*-ər-NAY-lee-ə): from Saturn, the Roman god of the harvest: any period of unrestrained merrymaking

10. vulcanize (VUL-kə-*niyz*): from Vulcan, the Roman god of fire and metalworking: to make harder and more substantial

SENTENCE FILL-IN

1. We have decided that it is impossible to cheat when that _____ professor gives an exam.

2. Automobile tires were greatly improved when the manufacturers learned to _____ rubber.

3. The instructor said that Lady Macbeth, though quite vicious, could be considered a _____ .

---

a (fat); ay (fate); ah (far); au (doubt); ch (church); e (self, care); ee (evening); ə (about); f (flag, phone); hw (while); i (fit); iy (kite); ŋ (link, sing); o (audio, corn); ow (open); oo (cook); oi (oil); sh (shoe, ambition); th (think); u (up, love); uw (ooze); yu (cure); yuw (youth, united); zh (pleasure)

4. _____ was once used to make terminally ill cancer patients more comfortable.

5. Whatever happened to those _____ women athletes the Soviet Union used to send to the Olympics?

6. Leland's _____ love of testing fate is likely to cost him dearly one of these days.

7. A demonstration of the young wrestler's almost _____ strength made his opponent tremble with fear.

8. As was expected, a weekend _____ followed the graduation ceremony.

9. The gay and lively tones of the _____ summoned one and all to the circus.

10. In recent years, much of the literature of _____ has become tasteless pornography.

MATCHING

_____ 1. vulcanize

_____ 2. Amazonian

_____ 3. morphine

_____ 4. Antaean

_____ 5. Icarian

_____ 6. Argus-eyed

_____ 7. heroine

_____ 8. calliope

_____ 9. saturnalia

_____10. erotica

a. a keyboard musical instrument with a series of steam whistles
b. foolishly daring
c. a drug that reduces pain and induces sleep
d. to make harder and more substantial
e. any period of unrestrained merrymaking
f. the major female character in a novel or play
g. art and literature treating the subject of sexual love
h. characteristic of a large, powerful, aggressive woman
i. almost invincible; possessing superhuman strength
j. always awake, vigilant, and observant

Words from Names in Mythology (5)

WORD LIST

1. aphrodisiac (*af*-rə-DIZ-ee-*ak*):   from Aphrodite, the Greek goddess of love, beauty, and fertility: any substance that arouses sexual desire

2. Cassandra (kə-SAN-drə):   from Cassandra, a Trojan princess to whom Apollo gave the powers of prophecy: one who constantly predicts disaster but is ignored

3. cyclopean (*siy*-klə-PEE-ən):   from the Cyclops, a race of Titans with a single eye in the middle of the forehead: gigantic, massive, enormous

4. Daedalean (di-DAY-lee-ən):   from Daedalus, father of Icarus and a very skillful artisan and builder: intricate, skillful, ingenious

5. Elysian (i-LIZH-ən):   from Elysium, the happy otherworld for heroes favored by the gods: blissfully happy; delightful

6. herculean (*hur*-kyə-LEE-ən):   from Hercules, son of Zeus and mightiest of all Greco-Roman heroes: requiring enormous strength, size, courage

7. Janus-faced (JAY-nəs-*fayst*):   from Janus, the two-faced (looking in opposite directions) Roman god of beginnings and endings: two-faced, deceitful, or unfaithful

8. narcissism (NAHR-sə-*siz*-əm):   from Narcissus, the beautiful son of Cephisus and Liriope who fell in love with his own reflection: excessive love of self, especially of one's own appearance

9. Promethean (prə-MEE-thee-ən):   from Prometheus, a Titan who ridiculed the gods and delivered fire to humankind: courageously creative; boldly original

10. satyric (sə-TIR-ik):   from the Satyrs, sylvan deities attendant upon Dionysus, having the appearance of men but with the legs and feet of goats: related to a man greatly desirous of sexual pleasures; lecherous

SENTENCE FILL-IN

1. A sort of semiprofessional _____, Truman spends his afternoons on the street corner prophesying the end of the world.

2. Professor Evans has concocted a whole series of _____ exercises for testing the abilities of her students.

3. Nothing less than a _____ effort is going to be required to feed the world's starving people.

---

a (fat);   ay (fate);   ah (far);   au (doubt);   ch (church);   e (self, care);   ee (evening);   ə (about);   f (flag, phone);   hw (while);   i (fit);   iy (kite);   ŋ (link, sing);   o (audio, corn);   ow (open);   oo (cook);   oi (oil);   sh (shoe, ambition);   th (think);   u (up, love);   uw (ooze);   yu (cure);   yuw (youth, united);   zh (pleasure)

4. It was forced abstinence that brought Ted to his present _____ state.

5. The number of mirrors in the average home suggests that there is a little _____ in each of us.

6. Affection often proves a more effective _____ than does any potion or drug.

7. It requires almost _____ courage and cleverness for a private individual to oppose a giant corporation.

8. Every professional football team seems to have dozens of _____ creatures.

9. I was amazed that anyone would believe the stories of this _____ traitor.

10. The novel presented a marvelous _____ society in which everyone was happy.

MATCHING

_____ 1. satyric

_____ 2. aphrodisiac

_____ 3. Promethean

_____ 4. Cassandra

_____ 5. narcissism

_____ 6. cyclopean

_____ 7. Janus-faced

_____ 8. Daedalean

_____ 9. herculean

_____ 10. Elysian

a. intricate, skillful, ingenious
b. excessive love of self, especially of one's own appearance
c. two-faced, deceitful, or unfaithful
d. requiring enormous strength, size, courage
e. related to a man greatly desirous of sexual pleasures; lecherous
f. gigantic, massive, enormous
g. one who constantly predicts disaster, but is ignored
h. any substance that arouses sexual desire
i. courageously creative; boldly original
j. blissfully happy; delightful

Words from Names in History (6)

WORD LIST

1. bedlam (BED-ləm):   from St. Mary of Bethlehem, an old London insane asylum: any situation of total confusion
2. boycott (BOI-*kaht*):   from Charles Cunningham Boycott, a nineteenth-century British army officer and landlord who was ostracized by his Irish tenants: joining in a group and refusing to do business with
3. chauvinism (SHOW-və-*niz*-əm):   from Nicholas Chauvin, a French soldier blindly devoted to Napoleon: excessive devotion to one's own country or group
4. gasconade (*gas*-kə-NAYD):   from the proud people of Gascony, a province in southwestern France: extravagantly boastful talk
5. Gothic (GAHTH-ik):   from the Goths, the barbarian people who conquered the Roman Empire: characterized by an absence of civility; rude and barbarous
6. jeremiad (*jer*-ə-MIY-əd):   from Jeremiah, an Old Testament Hebrew prophet of doom: a long, sorrowful complaint
7. pasteurize (PAS-chə-*riyz*):   from Louis Pasteur, a nineteenth-century French chemist and bacteriologist: to destroy or control the disease-producing bacteria in liquids
8. quisling (KWIZ-liŋ):   from Vidkun Quisling, a Norwegian army officer who betrayed his country to the Nazis: a foul traitor
9. sabotage (SAB-ə-*tahzh*):   from *sabots,* wooden shoes once worn by (unhappy) machine operators in Europe: an intentional underhanded interference with the operations of anything
10. sardonic (sahr-DAHN-ik):   from *Herba sardonica,* a poisonous plant native to Sardinia: bitterly sneering and sarcastic

SENTENCE FILL-IN

1. The great Norman cathedrals notwithstanding, all things _____ were once thought rude and vulgar.

2. Given the opportunity, this _____ would sell our enemies the Statue of Liberty.

3. The terrorists have embarked on a scheme to _____ as many factories in the Common Market countries as possible.

---

a (f*a*t);   ay (f*a*te);   ah (f*a*r);   au (d*ou*bt);   ch (*ch*ur*ch*);   e (s*e*lf, c*a*re);   ee (*e*vening);   ə (*a*bout);   f (*f*lag, *ph*one);   hw (*wh*ile);   i (f*i*t);   iy (k*i*te);   ŋ (li*n*k, si*ng*);   o (*au*dio, c*o*rn);   ow (*o*pen);   oo (c*oo*k);   oi (*oi*l);   sh (*sh*oe, ambi*ti*on);   th (*th*ink);   u (*u*p, l*o*ve);   uw (*oo*ze);   yu (c*u*re);   yuw (*you*th, *u*nited);   zh (plea*s*ure)

4. Is it really true that the Arab oil _____ brought the giant American oil companies to their knees?

5. The new dean's penchant for _____ suggests that his conceit outdoes his accomplishments.

6. Many people find Clinton's _____ wit unbearable.

7. To a foreign visitor, an American political convention must seem like total

_____ .

8. Many brewers say that when you _____ beer you ruin its natural taste.

9. Male _____ has become an accusation that includes numerous supposed faults among the male population.

10. While touring the pubs, we were woefully entertained by one long, drunken

_____ after another.

MATCHING

_____ 1. sardonic

_____ 2. bedlam

_____ 3. sabotage

_____ 4. boycott

_____ 5. quisling

_____ 6. chauvinism

_____ 7. pasteurize

_____ 8. gasconade

_____ 9. jeremiad

_____ 10. Gothic

a. any situation of total confusion
b. joining in a group and refusing to do business with
c. excessive devotion to one's own country or group
d. a foul traitor
e. extravagantly boastful talk
f. characterized by an absence of civility; rude and barbarous
g. a long, sorrowful complaint
h. to destroy or control the disease-producing bacteria in liquids
i. bitterly sneering and sarcastic
j. an intentional underhanded interference with the operations of anything

Words from Names in History (7)

WORD LIST

1. bedouin (BED-uw-in): from the Bedouins, ancient tribes of nomadic desert Arabs: a person who wanders from place to place

2. bogus (BOW-gəs): from a man named Borghese, who in the nineteenth century spread counterfeit money around the American West: not the real thing

3. cabal (kə-BAL): from *C*lifford, *A*shley, *B*uckingham, *A*rlington, and *L*auderdale—a group of political schemers under Charles II of England: a small group of political subversives

4. cynical (SIN-i-kəl): from the Cynics, a group of ancient Greek philosophers: always suspicious of people's motives; sarcastic

5. epicurean (*ep-ə-kyu-REE-ən*): from Epicurus, a Greek philosopher who advocated pleasure through temperance: devoted to such sensuous pleasures as rich food and drink, as well as to general luxury

6. grangerize (GRAYN-jə-*riyz*): from the Reverend James Granger, an eighteenth-century Englishman who illustrated his own book by clipping pictures out of other books: to clip pictures and illustrations out of (library) books; to mutilate (books)

7. jezebel (JEZ-ə-*bel*): from Jezebel, the wicked woman in the Bible who married Ahab, a king of Israel: a wicked, scheming, or shameless woman

8. martinet (*mahr*-tən-ET): from General Jean Martinet, a seventeenth-century French drillmaster and inventor of a system of military drill: a very strict disciplinarian

9. pharisaical (*far*-ə-SAY-i-kəl): from the Biblical Pharisees, a very strict ancient Hebrew sect: pretending to be more moral (spiritual) than you are; self-righteous; hypocritical

10. solecism (SAHL-ə-*siz*-əm): from the corrupt speech of the ancient people of Soloi, a city in Cilicia: a violation of either conventional language usage or good manners

SENTENCE FILL-IN

1. Familiarity with our tax laws is enough to make anyone _____ about government.

2. Our new football coach is a real _____; he even calls our homes at night to see whether we are in.

---

a (fat); ay (fate); ah (far); au (doubt); ch (church); e (self, care); ee (evening); ə (about); f (flag, phone); hw (while); i (fit); iy (kite); ŋ (link, sing); o (audio, corn); ow (open); oo (cook); oi (oil); sh (shoe, ambition); th (think); u (up, love); uw (ooze); yu (cure); yuw (youth, united); zh (pleasure)

3. If you trust this scheming _____, she is likely to break more than your heart.

4. Thad has lived the life of a _____, never staying in one place longer than a year or so.

5. Our instructors have repeatedly warned us not to _____ library books.

6. The speaker's _____ pretenses of piety annoyed most of the divinity students.

7. This embezzler has also made thousands of dollars selling _____ stock certificates.

8. A rather distinguished _____ of unseated senators is rumored to be plotting the overthrow of the government.

9. "I seen him" is an example of an irritating little _____.

10. Collins has an expense account that allows him to enjoy many of the _____ pleasures of life while he is on the road.

MATCHING

_____ 1. solecism

_____ 2. bedouin

_____ 3. pharisaical

_____ 4. bogus

_____ 5. martinet

_____ 6. cabal

_____ 7. jezebel

_____ 8. cynical

_____ 9. grangerize

_____ 10. epicurean

a. a violation of either conventional language usage or good manners

b. a wicked, scheming, or shameless woman

c. a very strict disciplinarian

d. pretending to be more moral (spiritual) than you really are; self-righteous; hypocritical

e. devoted to such sensuous pleasures as rich food and drink, as well as to general luxury

f. to clip pictures and illustrations out of (library) books; to mutilate (books)

g. always suspicious of other people's motives; sarcastic

h. a small group of political subversives

i. not the real thing

j. a person who wanders from place to place

Words from Names in History (8)

WORD LIST

1. billingsgate (BIL-iŋz-*gayt*): from the Billingsgate, an old entrance to London and a nearby fish market: very foul (vulgar) language

2. blarney (BLAHR-nee): from (kissing) the Blarney Stone at Blarney Castle in County Cork, Ireland: flattering (smooth) cajolery; coaxing chatter

3. Fabian (FAY-bee-ən): from Quintus Fabius Maximus, a Roman general who defeated Hannibal by the use of a delaying strategy: seeking victory by means that avoid direct confrontation

4. gimlet (GIM-lit): from Sir. T. O. Gimlette, a nineteenth-century British naval surgeon and inventor of a "healthy" cocktail: a drink of gin, lime juice, and soda water

5. Machiavellian (*mak*-ee-ə-VEL-ee-ən): from Niccolò Machiavelli, a sixteenth-century Florentine statesman and author of *The Prince*: related, generally, to all types of political craftiness or duplicity

6. mausoleum (*mo*-sə-LEE-əm): from the structure built at Halicarnassus to honor Mausolus, the ancient king of Caria: a stately or ornate tomb

7. nimrod (NIM-rahd): from Nimrod, the mighty hunter in the Book of Genesis: a hunter

8. philistine (FIL-is-*teen*): from the Biblical Philistines, a barbarous people who often made war on the Israelites: a narrow person who is smugly indifferent to culture

9. solon (SOW-lən): from Solon, an astute early sixth-century B.C. Athenian statesman: a wise lawmaker

10. sybarite (SIB-ə-*riyt*): from Sybaris, an ancient Greek city noted for its great wealth and luxury: a person excessively devoted to pleasure and self-indulgence

SENTENCE FILL-IN

1. The governor's new museum looks more like a _____ than a place very many people would want to visit.

2. Though I ordered a martini, the new waitress mistakenly brought me a _____ .

3. Many people find Thomas's cheerful _____ very entertaining.

4. The _____ who framed our Constitution were farsighted men.

---

a (f*a*t); ay (f*a*te); ah (f*a*r); au (d*ou*bt); ch (*ch*ur*ch*); e (s*e*lf, c*a*re); ee (*e*v*e*ning); ə (*a*bout); f (*f*lag, *ph*one); hw (*wh*ile); i (f*i*t); iy (k*i*te); ŋ (li*nk*, si*ng*); o (*au*dio, c*or*n); ow (*o*pen); oo (c*oo*k); oi (*oi*l); sh (*sh*oe, ambi*ti*on); th (*th*ink); u (*u*p, l*o*ve); uw (*oo*ze); yu (c*u*re); yuw (*you*th, *u*nited); zh (plea*s*ure)

5. Our young _____ tripped on a vine and shot himself in the foot with his hunting rifle.

6. What a _____ Hadley is; he says he despises anything with the taint of artiness about it.

7. The use of _____ in public seems an unfortunate circumstance of urban life.

8. A _____ political leader will do whatever is necessary to appease the greatest number of people.

9. This young _____ seems interested in nothing that does not provide instant gratification.

10. In a world that understands only unadorned power, _____ diplomacy is seldom effective.

MATCHING

_____ 1. sybarite

_____ 2. billingsgate

_____ 3. solon

_____ 4. blarney

_____ 5. philistine

_____ 6. Fabian

_____ 7. nimrod

_____ 8. gimlet

_____ 9. mausoleum

_____ 10. Machiavellian

a. a drink of gin, lime juice, and soda water

b. seeking victory by means that avoid direct confrontation

c. a person excessively devoted to pleasure and self-indulgence

d. a narrow person who is smugly indifferent to culture

e. flattering (smooth) cajolery; coaxing chatter

f. a wise lawmaker

g. related, generally, to all types of political craftiness or duplicity

h. very foul (vulgar) language

i. a hunter

j. a stately or ornate tomb

Words from Names in History (9)

WORD LIST

1. cicerone (*sis*-ə-ROW-nee):   from Marcus Tullius Cicero, an eloquent Roman statesman and orator: a guide who explains too thoroughly

2. derrick (DER-ik):   from Godfrey Derrick, a seventeenth-century hangman at Tyburn prison just outside London: a towerlike framework (apparatus) for lifting heavy objects

3. gerrymander (JER-i-*man*-dər):   from the political shenanigans that took place in Essex County, Massachusetts, under Governor Elbridge Gerry (1810–1812): to manipulate a (political) situation in order to gain an edge

4. Judas goat (JUW-dəs-*gowt*):   from Judas Iscariot, betrayer of Christ: one which leads its own kind to slaughter

5. mackintosh (MAK-in-*tahsh*):   from Charles Macintosh, nineteenth-century Scottish inventor of a waterproof coat: a heavy raincoat

6. maverick (MAV-ər-ik):   from Samuel Maverick, a nineteenth-century Texas rancher who didn't brand his calves: one who belongs to no established (political) group

7. pasquinade (*pas*-kwə-NAYD):   from Pasquino, a tailor of caustic wit who lived at Rome in the fifteenth century: satirical (public) ridicule; a lampoon

8. platonic (plə-TAHN-ik):   from Plato, the Greek philosopher: related to that which is mental or spiritual rather than physical or sexual

9. Spartan (SPAHR-tən):   from the inhabitants of ancient Sparta, the warlike city-state noted for its military excellence: hardy, severe, disciplined; tending to hostility

10. titian (TISH-ən):   from a particular color used by Titian, a sixteenth-century Venetian painter: auburn; a reddish golden brown

SENTENCE FILL-IN

1. Though something of a political _____, Pierre Trudeau managed to remain the Canadian prime minister for more than a decade.

2. How was the state representative able to _____ his district into such a strange configuration?

3. Norman's consummate ability at _____ makes him a difficult person to oppose in public.

---

a (*f*a*t*); ay (*f*a*te*); ah (*f*ar*); au (*d*ou*bt); ch (*ch*urch*); e (*s*e*lf, c*are*); ee (*ev*ening); ə (*ab*out*); f (*f*lag, *ph*one); hw (*wh*ile); i (*f*i*t*); iy (*k*i*te*); ŋ (*li*nk, *si*ng); o (*au*dio, *c*orn*); ow (*op*en*); oo (*c*oo*k*); oi (*oil*); sh (*sh*oe, ambi*ti*on*); th (*th*ink); u (*u*p, l*ove*); uw (*ooze*); yu (*c*u*re*); yuw (*y*outh, *u*nited*); zh (*pleasure*)

4. On Monday, a real _____-haired beauty sat for our oils class.

5. The energetic _____ simply wore everyone out with his elaborate narratives.

6. This _____ would lead his own brother to destruction if the money were right.

7. Life in the Orkney Islands off the northeastern coast of Scotland offers a very _____ existence.

8. It is small wonder—because of the damp climate—that a Scotsman invented and developed the _____.

9. What began innocently enough as a _____ relationship between two nice young people concluded as a tempestuous romance.

10. When the oil well finally came in, the entire _____ was blown away.

MATCHING

_____ 1. titian

_____ 2. cicerone

_____ 3. Spartan

_____ 4. derrick

_____ 5. platonic

_____ 6. gerrymander

_____ 7. pasquinade

_____ 8. Judas goat

_____ 9. maverick

_____ 10. mackintosh

a. a towerlike framework (apparatus) for lifting heavy objects

b. related to that which is mental or spiritual rather than physical or sexual

c. satirical (public) ridicule; a lampoon

d. a guide who explains too thoroughly

e. auburn; a reddish golden brown

f. a heavy raincoat

g. one which leads its own kind to slaughter

h. hardy, severe, disciplined; tending to hostility

i. to manipulate a (political) situation in order to gain an edge

j. one who belongs to no established (political) group

Words from Names in History (10)

WORD LIST

1. bowdlerize (BAUD-lə-*riyz*): from Thomas Bowdler, a nineteenth-century English editor who published a severely expurgated edition of Shakespeare: to remove supposedly objectionable passages from a published text

2. cardigan (KAHR-də-gən): from the Seventh Earl of Cardigan, an English general who dressed his troops rather nicely: a knitted sweater (jacket) that opens down the front

3. cretin (KREE-tin): from the Swiss-French application of the term "Christian" to certain deformed people to distinguish them from brutes: a dense, stupid person

4. Diogenic (*diy*-ə-JEN-ik): from Diogenes, an ancient Greek Cynic philosopher: cynical, churlish, independent

5. helot (HEL-ət): from the people of ancient Helos, who were enslaved by the Spartans: a member of the lowest (servile) classes; serf; slave

6. hooliganism (HUW-lə-gə-*niz*-əm): from Patrick Hooligan, a nineteenth-century ruffian who lived in Southwark, England, and worked as a bouncer in pubs: general rowdiness by a group of ruffians

7. jackstraw (JAK-stro): from Jack Straw, one of the leaders of the Peasants' Revolt in 1381: a generally worthless character

8. laconic (lə-KAHN-ik): from the people of ancient Laconia, noted for their brevity of speech: given to wasting as few words as possible

9. macadamized (mə-KAD-ə-*miyzd*): from John L. McAdam, a nineteenth-century Scottish engineer who invented a method for paving roads: paved with layers of ground stone bound with tar

10. spoonerism (SPUW-nə-*riz*-əm): from the Reverend William A. Spooner, an English clergyman who often transposed the initial sounds of words placed near each other (as, "God save our queer old dean" for "God save our dear old Queen"): transposition of the initial sounds in words placed near each other

SENTENCE FILL-IN

1. Calvin's _____ outlook makes him suspicious of most things.

2. Leslie confused the tale with a _____, saying "Cinderella slopped her dripper."

---

a (fat);   ay (fate);   ah (far);   au (doubt);   ch (church);   e (self, care);   ee (evening);   ə (about);   f (flag, phone);   hw (while);   i (fit);   iy (kite);   ŋ (link, sing);   o (audio, corn);   ow (open);   oo (cook);   oi (oil);   sh (shoe, ambition);   th (think);   u (up, love);   uw (ooze);   yu (cure);   yuw (youth, united);   zh (pleasure)

3. "What possible use could this _____ have for expensive jewelry!" shouted the king.

4. Few publishers would bother to _____ a book today, no matter what sort of indelicate material it might contain.

5. Professor Tully—a male chauvinist if ever there was one—called the young woman a

_____, saying that he was surprised she had remembered where the class met.

6. Destructive _____ seems to have become a type of entertainment for many of the city's young ruffians.

7. After twenty years of complaining, we succeeded in getting the road _____ last fall.

8. Everyone knows that this _____ isn't worth the powder it would take to blow him up.

9. I bought a handsome wool _____ at a mill in Scotland.

10. Marian has become so _____ that she hardly speaks to anyone other than her family.

MATCHING

_____ 1. spoonerism

_____ 2. bowdlerize

_____ 3. macadamized

_____ 4. cardigan

_____ 5. laconic

_____ 6. cretin

_____ 7. jackstraw

_____ 8. Diogenic

_____ 9. hooliganism

_____ 10. helot

a. a dense, stupid person
b. general rowdiness by a group of ruffians
c. paved with layers of ground stone bound with tar
d. to remove supposedly objectionable passages from a published text
e. a knitted sweater (jacket) that opens down the front
f. cynical, churlish, independent
g. a member of the lowest (servile) classes; serf; slave
h. a generally worthless character
i. given to wasting as few words as possible
j. transposition of the initial sounds in words placed near each other

Words from Names in History (11)

WORD LIST

1. Byzantine (BIZ-ən-*teen*):   from the Byzantine Empire of Eastern Europe between the fourth and fifteenth centuries: artistically and architecturally elaborate, decorative, and colorful

2. colossal (kə-LAHS-əl):   from the Colossus of Rhodes, a statue of Apollo: huge, enormous, or extraordinary

3. draconian (dray-KOW-nee-ən):   from Draco, an Athenian statesman and severe lawgiver: unusually severe and cruel; rigorous

4. Hobson's choice (HAHB-sənz-*chois*):   from Thomas Hobson, a seventeenth-century owner of a livery stable in Cambridge, England, who always made customers take the horse nearest to the door: no choice at all

5. lesbian (LEZ-bee-ən):   from the Greek island of Lesbos and the suspected homosexuality of its female inhabitants: a homosexual woman

6. meander (mee-AN-dər):   from the Menderes River (*Maeander* in Latin) in Asia Minor: to wander about aimlessly or to stray off course

7. puritanical (*pyur-ə-TAN-i-kəl*):   from the Puritans, a sixteenth-century Protestant sect in reaction against the Church of England: very rigid (unyielding) in moral matters; religiously strict

8. sub rosa (sub-ROW-zə):   from the ancient practice of hanging a rose near the door of a room where a confidential meeting was being held: performed privately or in strict confidence

9. tawdry (TO-dree):   from Saint Audrey, an Anglo-Saxon princess who in her youth wore golden chains and necklaces: cheap, ornate, or showy

10. vandalism (VAN-də-*liz*-əm):   from the Vandals, fifth-century plunderers of Rome: malicious and wanton destruction of public or private property

SENTENCE FILL-IN

1. I can see no reason why delegates from our own party would want to hold a

   _____ meeting.

2. On a casual summer's day it is pleasant to _____ through an old meadow.

---

a (*fat*); ay (*fate*); ah (*far*); au (*doubt*); ch (*church*); e (*self, care*); ee (*evening*); ə (*about*); f (*flag, phone*); hw (*while*); i (*fit*); iy (*kite*); ŋ (*link, sing*); o (*audio, corn*); ow (*open*); oo (*cook*); oi (*oil*); sh (*shoe, ambition*); th (*think*); u (*up, love*); uw (*ooze*); yu (*cure*); yuw (*youth, united*); zh (*pleasure*)

3. Such a _____ system of conditioning will not work with a team of professional athletes.

4. _____ has become so commonplace in big cities that many businesses now budget for it.

5. I would say the mistake was a _____ one; it resulted in the destruction of the entire west wing of the factory.

6. The question before the school board was whether an avowed _____ would be allowed to continue teaching in the elementary school.

7. Discount stores make millions selling their _____ trinkets.

8. We found four perfectly preserved _____ vases about sixteen feet below the surface.

9. These children were reared in such _____ surroundings that they had never heard anyone swear.

10. In recent elections, many people have viewed the choice between candidates as little

better than a _____.

MATCHING

_____ 1. vandalism

_____ 2. Byzantine

_____ 3. tawdry

_____ 4. colossal

_____ 5. sub rosa

_____ 6. draconian

_____ 7. puritanical

_____ 8. Hobson's choice

_____ 9. meander

_____10. lesbian

a. unusually severe and cruel; rigorous
b. no choice at all
c. a homosexual woman
d. very rigid (unyielding) in moral matters; religiously strict
e. cheap, ornate, or showy
f. malicious and wanton destruction of public or private property
g. performed privately or in strict confidence
h. to wander about aimlessly or to stray off course
i. artistically and architecturally elaborate, decorative, and colorful
j. huge, enormous, or extraordinary

Words from Names in Literature (12)

WORD LIST

1. Babbitt (BAB-it):   from George Babbitt in the novel *Babbitt* by Sinclair Lewis: a person concerned mainly with business and position, caring little for art or culture

2. buffoon (bə-FUWN):   from a clown in medieval comedies who puffed out his cheeks and then let them collapse with great noise: a jester or a witless individual

3. jabberwocky (JAB-ər-*wahk*-ee):   from a poem in Lewis Carroll's *Through the Looking Glass*: meaningless jibberish

4. malapropism (MAL-ə-prahp-*iz*-əm):   from Mrs. Malaprop in the play *The Rivals* by Richard Sheridan: a ridiculous misuse of one word for another similar (sounding) word

5. Micawberish (mi-KAH-bər-ish):   from Mr. Wilkins Micawber in the novel *David Copperfield* by Charles Dickens: hopelessly cheerful and optimistic

6. odyssey (AHD-ə-see):   from Odysseus in Homer's epic *The Odyssey*: an extended journey

7. Pickwickian (pik-WIK-ee-ən):   from Mr. Samuel Pickwick in Charles Dickens's *The Pickwick Papers*: generally kind, simple, and endearing

8. quixotic (kwik-SAHT-ik):   from Don Quixote in the novel *Don Quixote de la Mancha* by Cervantes: extravagantly romantic, idealistic, chivalrous

9. Shangri-la (*shaŋ*-grə-LAH):   from the imaginary land of James Hilton's novel *Lost Horizon*: an idyllic (hidden) paradise

10. Uncle Tomism (TAHM-*iz*-əm):   from Uncle Tom in the novel *Uncle Tom's Cabin* by Harriet Beecher Stowe: a black person's showing constant deference to white people

SENTENCE FILL-IN

1. I'm afraid the seminar consisted of little more than a lot of _____ about how we should all try to live up to our potential.

2. Wasn't it just a little _____ of you to spread your dinner jacket out for the lady to wipe her feet on?

3. Life itself might be thought of as a rather long _____.

---

a (fat);   ay (fate);   ah (far);   au (doubt);   ch (church);   e (self, care);   ee (evening);   ə (about);   f (flag, phone);   hw (while);   i (fit);   iy (kite);   ŋ (link, sing);   o (audio, corn);   ow (open);   oo (cook);   oi (oil);   sh (shoe, ambition);   th (think);   u (up, love);   uw (ooze);   yu (cure);   yuw (youth, united);   zh (pleasure)

7. As a youth I often swam _____ in a mountain lake.

8. The relationship eventually became a _____ from which neither of them knew how to withdraw.

9. Unless the people revolt _____, we will never have real tax reform.

10. Though today a _____ power, Great Britain still retains much of its old imperial charm.

MATCHING

_____ 1. par excellence

_____ 2. affaire d'amour

_____ 3. naiveté

_____ 4. au naturel

_____ 5. ennui

_____ 6. cri de coeur

_____ 7. en masse

_____ 8. cul-de-sac

_____ 9. déjeuner

_____ 10. déclassé

a. a general feeling of weariness or boredom

b. naked; cooked and served simply

c. any impassioned utterance or protest

d. a (passionate) love affair

e. a blind alley; a situation from which there seems no escape

f. reduced to a lower class; losing social status

g. a late breakfast or early lunch

h. superior to all others; beyond comparison

i. in a body; everyone together

j. artless simplicity or innocence

Foreign Expressions (4)

WORD LIST

1. au courant (*ow*-kuw-RAHN) F: with the (current) times; up-to-date and informed
2. carpe diem (*kahr*-pe-DEE-əm) L: seize the day; make the most of the present
3. chargé d'affaires (shahr-ZHAY-də-FER) F: a diplomat of subordinate rank but some authority
4. danse macabre (*dahns*-mah-KÂH-br') F: allegorical representation of Death leading people to the grave
5. démodé (*day*-mo-DAY) F: outmoded or out of fashion
6. diablerie (dee-AH-blə-ree) F: dealing with devils; fiendish wickedness; mischief
7. esprit de corps (es-PREE-də-KOR) F: a mutual sense of pride and honor among a group of people
8. haute couture (*owt*-kuw-TÛR) F: high fashion; clothing created by leading designers
9. mal de mer (*mâhl*-də-MER) F: seasickness
10. parvenu (PAHR-və-*nuw*) F: (a person) newly rich or powerful; an upstart

SENTENCE FILL-IN

1. The general _____ of the CIA has become more than an ordinary embarrassment to the American people.

2. We phoned the _____ at the embassy, but he was of little assistance.

3. Though everyone may be unique to some degree, each of us performs a little

   _____—and to the same end.

4. The outspoken ambassador was considered by many to be a diplomatic

   _____ when he first went to the United Nations.

5. That which is terribly _____ today may be just as terribly passé tomorrow.

---

a (f*a*t);   ay (f*a*te);   ah (f*a*r);   âh (m*a*l de mer);   au (d*o*ubt);   ah (*chur*ch);   e (s*e*lf, c*a*re);   ee (*e*vening);   ê (déj*eu*ner);   ə (*a*bout);   f (*f*lag, *ph*one);   hw (*wh*ile);   i (f*i*t);   iy (k*i*te);   ŋ (li*n*k, si*ng*);   o (*au*dio, c*or*n);   ô (sch*ö*n);   ow (*o*pen);   oo (c*oo*k);   oi (*oi*l);   sh (*sh*oe, ambi*ti*on);   th (*th*ink);   u (*u*p, l*o*ve);   û (mot j*u*ste);   uw (*oo*ze);   yu (c*u*re);   yuw (*you*th, *u*nited);   zh (plea*s*ure)

6. When the ship of state is in rough waters, everyone suffers from political

   _____.

7. Our puritanical backgrounds make many of us look askance on the contemporary

   _____ view of life.

8. There seemed to be a strong _____ among the players on the championship team.

9. Levi Strauss has almost succeeded in making denim an _____ fabric.

10. The _____ sentimentality of Victorian novels gets short shrift in the modern world.

MATCHING

_____ 1. parvenu

_____ 2. au courant

_____ 3. mal de mer

_____ 4. carpe diem

_____ 5. haute couture

_____ 6. chargé d'affaires

_____ 7. esprit de corps

_____ 8. démodé

_____ 9. diablerie

_____ 10. danse macabre

a. a mutual sense of pride and honor among a group of people
b. high fashion; clothing created by leading designers
c. seasickness
d. (a person) newly rich or powerful; an upstart
e. dealing with devils; fiendish wickedness; mischief
f. with the (current) times; up-to-date and informed
g. seize the day; make the most of the present
h. allegorical representation of Death leading people to the grave
i. outmoded or out of fashion
j. a diplomat of subordinate rank but some authority

Foreign Expressions (5)

WORD LIST

1. arriviste ($\widehat{a}h$-ree-VEEST) F: one who has recently gained power, wealth, or position (by questionable means); an upstart
2. beau geste (bow-ZHEST) F: a fine, magnanimous gesture—though often made for show
3. caveat (KAV-ee-*aht*) L: a warning or caution
4. chasseur (sha-SUR) F: a uniformed attendant serving the rich and powerful; a doorman, as at a hotel or club
5. déjà vu (*day*-zhah-VÛ) F: the mental illusion of having been somewhere, experienced something, before
6. fleur-de-lis (*flur*-də-LEE) F: the heraldic lily
7. haute cuisine (*owt*-kwee-ZEEN) F: finely prepared (expensive) food
8. persona non grata (pər-SOW-nə-nahn-GRAH-tə) L: an unwelcome or unacceptable person
9. potpourri (*pow*-poo-REE) F: a medley or anthology; a mixed bag
10. voyeur (VOI-yər) F: one who gets (sexual) gratification from watching others perform sexual acts

SENTENCE FILL-IN

1. An intense sense of _____ enveloped me as we approached the strangely familiar village.

2. Though the Hoof and Horn pretends to serve only _____, I have had several mediocre meals there.

3. For some time to come, the woman executive is likely to be considered an _____ by old-line middle-management types.

4. The place settings in the hotel dining room had a _____ pattern.

5. "Life," said the aging guru, "is a _____ of experiences, good and bad."

---

a (fat); ay (fate); ah (far); $\widehat{a}$h (mal de mer); au (doubt); ah (church); e (self, care); ee (evening); ê (déjeuner); ə (about); f (flag, phone); hw (while); i (fit); iy (kite); ŋ (link, sing); o (audio, corn); ô (schön); ow (open); oo (cook); oi (oil); sh (shoe, ambition); th (think); u (up, love); û (mot juste); uw (ooze); yu (cure); yuw (youth, united); zh (pleasure)

6. After the graceful _____ of offering the baton to his protégé, the retiring conductor left the stage quickly.

7. Some slick magazines make _____ of their readers.

8. You should take my little story as a friendly _____, not as idle gossip.

9. When his many indiscretions became known, the senator immediately became _____ around Washington.

10. Sharon felt very grand as the _____ opened the door of the taxi and escorted her into the hotel lobby.

MATCHING

_____ 1. voyeur

_____ 2. arriviste

_____ 3. potpourri

_____ 4. beau geste

_____ 5. persona non grata

_____ 6. caveat

_____ 7. haute cuisine

_____ 8. chasseur

_____ 9. fleur-de-lis

_____ 10. déjà vu

a. one who has recently gained wealth, power, or position (by questionable means); an upstart

b. a uniformed attendant serving the rich and powerful; a doorman, as at a hotel or club

c. one who gets (sexual) gratification from watching others perform sexual acts

d. a medley or anthology; a mixed bag

e. an unwelcome or unacceptable person

f. finely prepared (expensive) food

g. the heraldic lily

h. the illusion of having been somewhere, experienced something, before

i. a warning or caution

j. a fine, magnanimous gesture—though often made for show

Foreign Expressions (6)

WORD LIST

1. a priori (*ah*-pree-OR-ee) L: deductively, from general rule to specific instance; presumptive
2. affaire d'honneur (âh-FER-do-NÊR) F: a matter of honor, as a duel
3. cordon bleu (kor-*down*-BLÔ) F: any very high distinction; the person wearing the blue ribbon
4. dégagé (*day*-gah-ZHAY) F: casual and easy of manner; detached and emotionally uninvolved
5. dénouement (*day*-nuw-MAHN) F: a conclusion, outcome, or final solution
6. élan (ay-LAHN) F: dash, impetuousness, spirited self-assurance
7. ignis fatuus (IG-nis-FACH-uw-əs) L: an illusive light arising from swamp gas; thus, any delusive hope or idea
8. patois (PAT-*wah*) F: a specialized language, as of an occupation or field of study; jargon
9. roué (ruw-AY) F: one whose entire life has been devoted to sensuality
10. tour de force (*toor*-də-FOWRS) F: an exceptional performance, though (perhaps) done mostly for show

SENTENCE FILL-IN

1. Forget this _____ of proving beyond a doubt that there is life after death.

2. The government's _____ attitude toward the suffering of the aged is criminal.

3. Though Richard Burton's *Hamlet* couldn't be called a _____, it was good theater.

4. The climax of a play is followed by the _____.

5. The third match between the two ex-champions became a bloody _____.

6. There isn't anything this old _____ hasn't sampled at one time or another.

---

a (f*a*t); ay (f*a*te); ah (f*a*r); âh (m*a*l de mer); au (d*ou*bt); ah (*chur*ch); e (s*e*lf, c*a*re); ee (*e*vening); ê (déj*eu*ner); ə (*a*bout); f (*f*lag, *ph*one); hw (*wh*ile); i (f*i*t); iy (k*i*te); ŋ (li*n*k, si*ng*); o (*au*dio, c*o*rn); ô (sch*ö*n); ow (*o*pen); oo (c*oo*k); oi (*oi*l); sh (*sh*oe, ambi*ti*on); th (*th*ink); u (*u*p, l*o*ve); û (mot j*u*ste); uw (*oo*ze); yu (c*u*re); yuw (*you*th, *u*nited); zh (plea*s*ure)

7. Life's experiences generally temper the _____ of youth.

8. Your _____ statement of the youth's probable guilt because of his background was later disproved by the court.

9. The _____ of the legal profession is a kind of wordnoise that has caused many people to become disenchanted with our whole legal system.

10. The Nobel Prize is now the _____ of the literary world.

MATCHING

_____ 1. tour de force

_____ 2. affaire d'honneur

_____ 3. roué

_____ 4. a priori

_____ 5. patois

_____ 6. cordon bleu

_____ 7. ignis fatuus

_____ 8. dégagé

_____ 9. élan

_____10. dénouement

a. a conclusion, outcome, or final solution

b. a specialized language, as of an occupation or field of study; jargon

c. deductively, from general rule to specific instance; presumptive

d. a matter of honor, as a duel

e. dash, impetuousness, spirited self-assurance

f. one whose entire life has been devoted to sensuality

g. an exceptional performance, though (perhaps) done mostly for show

h. an illusive light arising from swamp gas; thus, any delusive hope or idea

i. casual and easy of manner; detached and emotionally uninvolved

j. any very high distinction; the person wearing the blue ribbon

Foreign Expressions (7)

WORD LIST

1. coup de grace (*kuw*-də-GRAHS) F: the death blow, delivered to terminate suffering
2. couturier (kuw-TOOR-ee-*ay*) F: a person who designs, makes, and markets women's clothes
3. gemütlich (gə-MÛT-likh) G: amiable and easy to get along with; congenial
4. in absentia (in-ab-SEN-shə) L: in the absence of (the person concerned)
5. joie de vivre (*zhwâh*-də-VEE-vr') F: the joy of living; a feeling of well-being
6. milieu (mil-YUW) F: a general environment or setting
7. nouveaux riches (*nuw*-vow-REESH) F: those people (collectively) who have recently become rich and are perhaps rather unpleasant about it
8. savoir-faire (SAV-wahr-FER) F: instinctive understanding of the right action under almost any circumstances
9. sobriquet (*sow*-brə-KAY) F: a nickname, sometimes humorous or affectionate
10. vox populi (VAHKS-PAHP-yə-*liy*) L: the voice of the people

SENTENCE FILL-IN

1. Though he often complained about it, Casper was unable to stop his classmates from calling him by the uncomplimentary _____.

2. A _____ atmosphere pervaded the old hall as we drank beer and sang songs.

3. Seemingly motivated by nothing more than _____, Judy makes it impossible for anyone around her to be sullen.

4. Toward the end of the eighteenth century, a class of _____ began to force its way into the upper strata of British society.

5. Though he has done a good many oils, the artist's real _____ is water colors.

---

a (fat);   ay (fate);   ah (far);   âh (mal de mer);   au (doubt);   ah (church);   e (self, care);   ee (evening);   ê (déjeuner);   ə (about);   f (flag, phone);   hw (while);   i (fit);   iy (kite);   ŋ (link, sing);   o (audio, corn);   ô (schön);   ow (open);   oo (cook);   oi (oil);   sh (shoe, ambition);   th (think);   u (up, love);   û (mot juste);   uw (ooze);   yu (cure);   yuw (youth, united);   zh (pleasure)

6. Ultimately, the political leader who ignores the _____ is doomed to failure.

7. At the close of World War II, the atom bomb dropped on Nagasaki was the _____ that ended Japanese resistance.

8. As a _____ for only the most wealthy, Emil ignores the mass market altogether.

9. Everyone envies Clark's _____; he always knows exactly what to say and do.

10. Though tried for his crimes _____, the former Nazi officer was later captured and executed.

MATCHING

_____ 1. vox populi

_____ 2. coup de grace

_____ 3. sobriquet

_____ 4. couturier

_____ 5. savoir-faire

_____ 6. gemütlich

_____ 7. nouveaux riches

_____ 8. in absentia

_____ 9. milieu

_____ 10. joie de vivre

a. a nickname, sometimes humorous or affectionate
b. the joy of living; a feeling of well-being
c. a general environment or setting
d. those people (collectively) who have recently become rich and are perhaps rather unpleasant about it
e. the voice of the people
f. instinctive understanding of the right action under almost any circumstances
g. amiable and easy to get along with; congenial
h. a person who designs, makes, and markets women's clothes
i. in the absence of (the person concerned)
j. the death blow, delivered to terminate suffering

Foreign Expressions (8)

WORD LIST

1. a posteriori (*ay*-pahs-*tir*-ee-OR-ee) L: inductively, a conclusion from experiences or observations
2. beau monde (*bow*-MOND) F: the fashionable world; high society
3. bon vivant (*bon*-vee-VAHN) F: one who lives in luxury and knows all about good food and drink
4. cause célèbre (KOZ-sə-LEB-r') F: a controversy attracting great public attention
5. caveat emptor (KAV-ee-*aht*-EMP-tor) L: let the buyer beware
6. coup d'état (*kuw*-day-TAH) F: a sudden, decisive overthrow of the government
7. de jure (di-JOOR-ee) L: according to the law; by legal right
8. élan vital (ay-LAHN-vee-TÂHL) F: the (creative) life force
9. noblesse oblige (now-BLES-ow-BLEEZH) F: the (moral) obligation of the rich to display honorable and charitable conduct
10. realpolitik (ray-AHL-*pow*-li-TEEK) G: realistic politics, based on the facts of power rather than on philosophical idealism

SENTENCE FILL-IN

1. Life's simple pleasures no longer appeal to the aging _____.

2. The same _____ that shapes a great maple also motivates the composer of a moving symphony.

3. An _____ judgment, based on years of experience, is more likely to be sound than a judgment made only on a so-called gut reaction.

4. Our changing relations with the Arab nations, particularly the oil producers, are a matter of _____, not egalitarian idealism.

5. There has never been a successful _____ in the United States.

6. The Equal Rights Amendment has been a _____ of major duration.

---

a (f*a*t); ay (f*a*te); ah (f*a*r); âh (m*a*l de mer); au (d*ou*bt); ah (*ch*ur*ch*); e (s*e*lf, c*a*re); ee (*e*vening); ê (déj*eu*ner); ə (*a*bout); f (*f*lag, *ph*one); hw (*wh*ile); i (f*i*t); iy (k*i*te); ŋ (li*nk*, si*ng*); o (*au*dio, c*or*n); ô (sch*ö*n); ow (*o*pen); oo (c*oo*k); oi (*oi*l); sh (*sh*oe, ambi*ti*on); th (*th*ink); u (*u*p, love); û (mot j*u*ste); uw (*oo*ze); yu (c*u*re); yuw (*you*th, *u*nited); zh (plea*s*ure)

7. Consumer groups are fighting the resurgent _____ attitude of many of the newer conglomerates.

8. These Indians claim _____ rights to many acres of oil-rich land.

9. As a gesture of _____, the Rockefeller Foundation subsidizes an occasional program on the public television network.

10. The _____ pretentions of the small midwestern community amused the visiting lecturer.

MATCHING

_____ 1. realpolitik

_____ 2. a posteriori

_____ 3. noblesse oblige

_____ 4. beau monde

_____ 5. élan vital

_____ 6. bon vivant

_____ 7. de jure

_____ 8. cause célèbre

_____ 9. coup d'état

_____ 10. caveat emptor

a. the fashionable world; high society
b. according to the law; by legal right
c. let the buyer beware
d. the (moral) obligation of the rich to display honorable and charitable conduct
e. realistic politics, based on the facts of power rather than on philosophical idealism
f. inductively, a conclusion from experiences or observations
g. one who lives in luxury and knows all about good food and drink
h. the (creative) life force
i. a controversy attracting great public attention
j. a sudden, decisive overthrow of the government

Foreign Expressions (9)

WORD LIST

1. affaire de coeur (âh-FER-də-KÊR) F: an affair of the heart; a (sentimental) love affair
2. bel-esprit (*bel*-es-PREE) F: a person of great wit and intellect
3. château (sha-TOW) F: a French feudal house; a large country house on an estate
4. dernier cri (*der-nyay*-KREE) F: the latest fashion; the last word
5. fait accompli (*fe*-tâh-kown-PLEE) F: an accomplished fact; something done which cannot be undone
6. modus operandi (MOW-dəs-*ahp*-ə-RAN-dee) L: mode (method) of operation
7. ne plus ultra (*nee-plus*-UL-trə) L: the highest point (summit) of achievement
8. pastiche (pas-TEESH) F: artistic, literary, or musical work that includes material from many sources; a mixture
9. soi-disant (*swâh*-dee-ZAHN) F: self-styled, so-called, would-be, pretended
10. Wunderkind (VOON-dər-*kint*) G: a wonderful child; a child prodigy

SENTENCE FILL-IN

1. For a time a few years ago, the waterbed was the _____ in bedroom hardware.

2. A good many antique-car buffs still think the Stanley Steamer was the

   _____ of American automotive engineering.

3. An engaging _____, Professor Molière transforms every lecture into an intellectual happening.

4. Though he is an apt little pianist, Henry is no _____.

5. The corporation's entire _____ is based on the goal of minimizing costs and maximizing profits.

6. Over the years, the relationship between Logan and his secretary has become an

   _____.

---

a (fat);   ay (fate);   ah (far);   âh (mal de mer);   au (doubt);   ah (church);   e (self, care);   ee (evening);   ê (déjeuner);   ə (about);   f (flag, phone);   hw (while);   i (fit);   iy (kite);   ŋ (link, sing);   o (audio, corn);   ō (schön);   ow (open);   oo (cook);   oi (oil);   sh (shoe, ambition);   th (think);   u (up, love);   û (mot juste);   uw (ooze);   yu (cure);   yuw (youth, united);   zh (pleasure)

7. Fortunately, we learned in time that the _____ divine had purchased his credentials from a mail-order diploma mill.

8. My medieval history instructor has built a replica of a French _____ a few miles from town.

9. The program was nostalgic, a _____ of a dozen old films.

10. Since the dissolution of the remedial reading program was a _____, there was no point in discussing the low literacy level of the students.

MATCHING

_____ 1. Wunderkind

_____ 2. affaire de coeur

_____ 3. soi-disant

_____ 4. bel-esprit

_____ 5. pastiche

_____ 6. château

_____ 7. ne plus ultra

_____ 8. dernier cri

_____ 9. modus operandi

_____ 10. fait accompli

a. artistic, literary, or musical work that includes material from many sources; a mixture

b. a French feudal house; a large country house on an estate.

c. an accomplished fact; something done which cannot be undone

d. the latest fashion; the last word

e. self-styled, so-called, would-be, pretended

f. a wonderful child; a child prodigy

g. an affair of the heart; a (sentimental) love affair

h. mode (method) of operation

i. the highest point (summit) of achievement

j. a person of great wit and intellect

Foreign Expressions (10)

WORD LIST

1. bonhomie (*bahn*-ə-MEE) F: an amiable, easygoing disposition; a good-natured person
2. de trop (də-TROW) F: too much; (one) too many; superfluous and therefore not wanted
3. ipso facto (IP-sow-FAK-tow) L: by that very fact (itself)
4. leitmotif (LIYT-mow-*teef*) G: a basic, underlying, recurrent theme
5. mot juste (mow-ZHÛST) F: the right word or the appropriate phrase
6. non sequitur (nahn-SEK-wi-tər) L: a conclusion that does not follow logically from the premise
7. pièce de résistance (*pyes*-də-ray-zee-STAHNS) F: the most important item, as in a meal, collection, program, or the like
8. pro bono publico (prow-BOW-now-PUB-li-kow) L: for the public good
9. pro forma (prow-FOR-mə) L: (only) as a matter of form; as a gesture
10. soigné (swah-NYAY) F: well arranged; in good taste; carefully dressed; stylish

SENTENCE FILL-IN

1. Such a clumsy _____ will not appear logical to anyone.

2. Everyone agreed that Ravel's *Bolero* was the _____ of the evening's entertainment.

3. Patricia displays such pleasant _____ that it is impossible not to like her.

4. For having admitted his hatred of the victim, Ronald was convicted _____ by his own words.

5. The _____ of the new president's opening address was an administration that would be responsive to student problems.

6. Such _____ praise was neither wanted nor appreciated.

---

a (*fat*); ay (*fate*); ah (*far*); âh (m*al* de mer); au (d*ou*bt); ah (*church*); e (s*elf*, c*are*); ee (*evening*); ê (*déjeu*ner); ə (*about*); f (*flag*, *ph*one); hw (*wh*ile); i (*fit*); iy (k*ite*); ŋ (li*nk*, si*ng*); o (*au*dio, c*or*n); ô (sch*ö*n); ow (*open*); oo (c*oo*k); oi (*oil*); sh (*sh*oe, ambi*ti*on); th (*th*ink); u (*up*, l*o*ve); û (mot j*u*ste); uw (*ooze*); yu (c*u*re); yuw (y*ou*th, *u*nited); zh (plea*s*ure)

7. An academic counselor's _____ advice should not be taken as doctrine.

8. By using the polite _____ "diplomat" to label the Labourite political hack, the member of Parliament drew a warm ovation from the conservative audience.

9. Pretending that your self-serving schemes are _____ only compounds your villainy.

10. So _____ an appearance suggests that the young man spends a measure of his time in front of the looking glass.

MATCHING

_____ 1. soigné

_____ 2. bonhomie

_____ 3. pro forma

_____ 4. de trop

_____ 5. pro bono publico

_____ 6. ipso facto

_____ 7. pièce de résistance

_____ 8. leitmotif

_____ 9. non sequitur

_____ 10. mot juste

a. too much; (one) too many; superfluous and therefore not wanted

b. for the public good

c. the right word or the appropriate phrase

d. well arranged; in good taste; carefully dressed; stylish

e. (only) as a matter of form; as a gesture

f. an amiable, easygoing disposition; a good-natured person

g. a basic, underlying, recurrent theme

h. a conclusion that does not follow logically from the premise

i. by that very fact (itself)

j. the most important item, as in a meal, collection, program, or the like

Foreign Expressions (11)

WORD LIST

1. au fait (ow-FAY) F: well-versed; informed; knowing the facts
2. boulevardier (*buwl*-vâhr-DYAY) F: a man-about-town
3. de rigueur (də-ree-GÊR) F: absolutely required by proper etiquette; indispensable
4. ex post facto (*eks-powst*-FAK-tow) L: after the fact; retroactive; retrospective
5. omertà (o-MER-tah) It: the code (within a group) of remaining silent to outsiders
6. raison d'état (re-*zown*-day-TAH) F: an explanation (reason) given by the state and often understandable only to the state
7. recherché (rə-SHER-shay) F: perhaps too exquisite and refined; out of the ordinary
8. soiree (swah-RAY) F: an evening party or social gathering
9. soupçon (suwp-SOWN) F: a slight trace or suggestion of
10. Weltschmerz (VELT-*shmertz*) G: a kind of sentimental pessimism toward life

SENTENCE FILL-IN

1. Custom-designed zodiac pendants were considered _____ at the International Astrological Convention.

2. _____ legislation resulted in the release of hundreds of people who had been jailed for the possession of small amounts of marijuana.

3. The spokesman certainly seemed _____ to me, his lack of formal education notwithstanding.

4. Such _____ taste in food and drink is unusual for one with so provincial a background.

5. The small-town _____ found himself intimidated by London.

6. More than a _____ of suspicion resulted when five of the doctor's patients contracted hepatitis.

7. The annual theatrical _____ is held before the opening of the first play of the season.

---

a (f*a*t);   ay (f*a*te);   ah (f*a*r);   âh (m*a*l de mer);   au (d*ou*bt);   ah (*chur*ch);   e (s*e*lf, c*a*re);   ee (*e*vening);   ê (déj*eu*ner);   ə (*a*bout);   f (*f*lag, *ph*one);   hw (*wh*ile);   i (f*i*t);   iy (k*i*te);   ŋ (li*nk*, si*ng*);   o (*au*dio, c*or*n);   ô (sch*ö*n);   ow (*o*pen);   oo (c*oo*k);   oi (*oi*l);   sh (*sh*oe, ambi*ti*on);   th (*th*ink);   u (*u*p, l*o*ve);   û (mot j*u*ste);   uw (*oo*ze);   yu (c*u*re);   yuw (*you*th, *u*nited);   zh (plea*s*ure)

337

8. The author's general optimism belies the _____ of his early novels.

9. The president's _____ for declaring martial law was that he wanted to protect the individual freedom of the people.

10. The residents of urban ghettos may be justified in viewing the code of _____ as their first defense against outside aggression by local political machines.

MATCHING

_____ 1. Weltschmerz

_____ 2. au fait

_____ 3. soupçon

_____ 4. boulevardier

_____ 5. soiree

_____ 6. de rigueur

_____ 7. recherché

_____ 8. ex post facto

_____ 9. raison d'état

_____ 10. omertà

a. the code (within a group) of remaining silent to outsiders

b. an explanation (reason) given by the state, and often understandable only to the state

c. an evening party or social gathering

d. a kind of sentimental pessimism toward life

e. well-versed; informed; knowing the facts

f. a man-about-town

g. absolutely required by proper etiquette; indispensable

h. after the fact; retroactive; retrospective

i. a slight trace or suggestion of

j. perhaps too exquisite and refined; out of the ordinary

Foreign Expressions (12)

WORD LIST

1. c'est la vie (*se*-lâh-VEE) F: that's life; such is life
2. coup de main (*kuw*-də-MAN) F: a sudden, vigorous (surprise) attack, as in war
3. memento mori (mə-MEN-tow-MOW-riy) L: any reminder of death, as a skull
4. nouveauté (*nuw*-vow-TAY) F: a novelty; the latest thing
5. outré (uw-TRAY) F: beyond the limits of convention; exaggerated or eccentric
6. postiche (po-STEESH) F: a substitute of inferior quality; a pretense or sham
7. quid pro quo (*kwid*-prow-KWOW) L: this for that; one thing in fair exchange for another
8. réchauffé (*ray*-show-FAY) F: a dish of warmed-over food scraps; any old (literary) work rehashed and published again
9. sine qua non (SIY-nee-kway-NAHN) L: a necessary and essential thing; an indispensable requirement
10. tabula rasa (TAB-yə-lə-RAH-sə) L: a mind not yet affected by experience; a clean slate

SENTENCE FILL-IN

1. We saw no greater _____ on our tour of Europe than the World War I battlefields in Flanders.

2. This legislative _____ will not take the place of a fair-housing bill.

3. Television programming is basically a _____ of old plots and themes that have long since lost all entertainment value.

4. "_____" was all Henri had to say when his wife left him for another man.

5. Your _____ behavior at the funeral shocked everyone.

6. This _____ procedure of plea bargaining in such major cases displeases many people who think the punishment should fit the crime.

7. A _____ launched before dawn drove the rebels from the castle.

---

a (*fat*); ay (*fate*); ah (*far*); âh (m*a*l de mer); au (d*ou*bt); ah (*church*); e (s*e*lf, c*a*re); ee (*evening*); ê (déj*eu*ner); ə (*about*); f (*flag*, *phone*); hw (*while*); i (f*i*t); iy (k*i*te); ŋ (li*n*k, si*ng*); o (*au*dio, c*o*rn); ô (sch*ö*n); ow (*open*); oo (c*oo*k); oi (*oil*); sh (*shoe*, ambi*tion*); th (*think*); u (*up*, l*o*ve); û (mot j*u*ste); uw (*ooze*); yu (*cure*); yuw (*youth*, *u*nited); zh (plea*s*ure)

8. The concept of genetic memory contradicts the idea that the mind is a
_____ at birth.

9. Films dramatizing the lives of liberated women are the _____ of the motion picture industry just now.

10. Mutual respect is a _____ for a happy and successful marriage.

MATCHING

_____ 1. tabula rasa

_____ 2. c'est la vie

_____ 3. sine qua non

_____ 4. coup de main

_____ 5. réchauffé

_____ 6. memento mori

_____ 7. quid pro quo

_____ 8. nouveauté

_____ 9. postiche

_____ 10. outré

a. beyond the limits of convention; exaggerated or eccentric

b. a substitute of inferior quality; a pretense or sham

c. this for that; one thing in fair exchange for another

d. a dish of warmed-over food scraps; any old (literary) work rehashed and published again

e. a mind not yet affected by experience; a clean slate

f. a necessary and essential thing; an indispensable requirement

g. that's life; such is life

h. a sudden, vigorous (surprise) attack, as in war

i. any reminder of death, as a skull

j. a novelty; the latest thing

Self-scoring Posttest

MULTIPLE CHOICE

Place the letter of the best answer in the blank space.

_____ 1. To *bludgeon* is to
   a. deny all connections with
   b. encourage the development of
   c. beat with a stick
   d. refer to indirectly

_____ 2. *Frugal* people are likely to be
   a. thrifty
   b. musically inclined
   c. quarrelsome
   d. hard working

_____ 3. A *calliope* is a
   a. tropical lizard
   b. hundred-eyed giant
   c. flat-bottomed boat
   d. musical instrument

_____ 4. Your *magnum opus* is your
   a. nemesis
   b. greatest accomplishment
   c. worst personal disaster
   d. residence

_____ 5. To *recant* is to
   a. pour back and forth
   b. ridicule openly
   c. disfigure beyond repair
   d. renounce former statements

_____ 6. *Garrulous* children are often
   a. pensive
   b. portly
   c. talkative
   d. retarded

_____ 7. A *roué* is likely to be a
   a. saint
   b. logician
   c. rascal
   d. composer

_____ 8. A *potpourri* is a
   a. hot broth
   b. mixed bag
   c. medieval hymn
   d. printed manuscript

_____ 9. A person who is *au courant* is
   a. approaching death
   b. confused
   c. generally friendly
   d. up-to-date

_____ 10. A *furtive* look is usually
   a. sexy
   b. stealthy
   c. questioning
   d. complacent

_____ 11. To *abridge* is to
   a. spread out
   b. condense
   c. postpone
   d. cross over

_____ 12. A *cicerone* is likely to
   a. cheat you of your money
   b. drink too much wine
   c. talk too much
   d. listen patiently to your problems